Stories from Candyland

Stories from Candyland

Candy Spelling

St. Martin's Press
New York

www.stmartins.com

Book design by Kathryn Parise

LIBRARY OF CONGRESS CATALOGING-IN-PUBLICATION DATA

Spelling, Candy.
    Stories from Candyland / Candy Spelling. — 1st ed.
        p. cm.
    ISBN-13: 978-0-312-57070-5
    ISBN-10: 0-312-57070-8
    1. Spelling, Candy.   2. Spelling, Aaron.   3. Television producers' and
directors' spouses—United States—Biography.   I. Title.
    PN1992.4.S64A3 2009
    791.4302'33092—dc22
    [B]
                                                                    20008054719

First Edition: April 2009

10   9   8   7   6   5   4   3   2   1

To Aaron,

My love . . . and the man who entertained
the world with great stories.
I hope my storytelling makes you proud.

Contents

✤

Contents

Acknowledgments

❧

I always thought writers lived the most solitary of lives. I know my late husband, Aaron Spelling, would often lock himself up in his office or get up in the middle of the night to write, and it never was a group activity.

When I started to write *Stories from Candyland,* the silence was deafening. I thought I had fun stories and one-of-a-kind experiences to relate but wasn't sure how I'd be able to tell them. Aaron Spelling had been a great storyteller. Candy Spelling was a good listener.

As soon as I began, I realized writing is a very collaborative experience. So many people helped me with this book, and I want to thank them.

First the dogs, starting with my Madison, who was there every night, all night, when I was at my computer telling my stories. I think my wheaten terrier stood, sat, and curled up by me to make sure she was included in the book. She is.

Next, here's a note to Madison's friends Izzy and Sarge:

It was while visiting my past and present I found a muse who knew just when to push, when to encourage, and when to laugh. Thanks, guys, for letting her spend hours on the phone listening to ideas and stories and, yes, a bit of grousing, all the things that go into writing a book. Among the pages of *Stories from Candyland,* I found a sweet and dear friend, your mom, Linda Dozoretz.

I'd like to thank my editor, Elizabeth Beier, at St. Martin's Press. You referred to me as an "archivist" and not a "collector" or "hoarder." I can't tell you the psychological good you did for me. When you giggled and said, "I know you have a fun book," that day at my house, I experienced a combination of excitement and fear that hasn't gone away. That's not bad, though. Thank you for all your help.

Sally Richardson and her team warmly welcomed me to the St. Martin's family. Michelle Richter, Steve Snider, John

Acknowledgments

Murphy, Ann Day, Courtney Fischer, Meg Drislane, Kathryn Parise, and Jenna Dolan were also great at navigating their first-time author through this project.

My thanks to Tina Brausam, Lu Ann Smith, Barbara Sloane, and Roberta Greene for their help on myriad details and for their goodwill in accommodating my crazy schedule and hours, and to Will Soper for his creativity and care of my precious photographs.

David Shapira introduced me to Elizabeth and St. Martin's and had great ideas for some of the chapters. Stephen Goldberg and Brian Wolf helped navigate through the legal issues. Jeanne Wolf's encouragement about telling my life stories means so much. I appreciate Kim Dower's helping me to overcome my shyness to tell these stories. I'm still a work in progress.

Thanks to Dr. Andrea Brandt, who helped me hum happier tunes.

I am blessed with friends who have been part of my life since the earliest days in school. To Nancy Blumenfeld, who has been my sister since I was five years old, plus my Mah-Jongg buddies Willy Erlicht, Fran, Sheila, Darlene, Linda, Lucy, Joyce, Kris, Wendy, Fabienne, Pitzie, and Cheryl. To the Simmons family, Denise, Danny, Victoria, and Laura, who have been such a major support for as long as I have known them. My Syrian sister, Ghada Irani, has graciously taken me everywhere in the world. I love her dearly. To Alicia

Acknowledgments

Rose and Paula Meehan, I appreciate the love, laughs, and inspiration. You told me I could write a book. I think I'm beginning to believe you.

I have a great personal team, too. Alana Voeller seemed to be spending more days making copies and air-expressing photos than she spent at home. Rodney Baer helped me find the items in the attic, then counted boxes, found descriptions, and assured me that I was as organized as I hoped I was.

Other special help came from Bob Dally, who not only decorates my homes but brightens my life; Beverly Callison, who remembered all the little things, which is why Aaron loved her; and Kevin Sasaki. Thank goodness he hired people with great memories.

I loved telling my son, Randy, about the stories I was relating and laughing with him at some of the memories and experiences our family shared. I love you, Randy.

Some of my inspiration came from knowing that I have two grandchildren, Liam Aaron and Stella Doreen, thanks to my daughter, Tori, and her husband, Dean. I wanted them to hear about their grandfather, grandmother, mother, and uncle and know how great life can be.

I truly appreciate all the support and encouragement from so many special people in my life. As in any "game," I look forward to the next move.

Introduction

I hadn't done a lot of writing in my life.

Growing up, I had learning disabilities before ADD and dyslexia had names, and my education was dedicated to pursuits such as being charming, polite, and fashionable, plus learning sewing, cooking, decorating, good posture, proper etiquette, dancing, and preparing to be the best wife ever.

Once I married Aaron Spelling and tried to be the best wife ever, I didn't think much about writing. I was married to the man who would become the most prolific producer and writer in television history. His influence helped define pop culture for decades. I was his collaborator, cheerleader, executive assistant, housekeeper, trophy wife, companion, and support, and I loved almost every minute of it.

After Aaron died in June 2006, I realized that much of my life's job was done. As Mrs. Aaron (Candy) Spelling, as etiquette suggested, I ran businesses, raised children, designed and built houses, and had my charitable work and many friends and activities—but Aaron had listened to me, communicated with me, had been my barometer for social, cultural, and political issues and much more.

I realized I could have a voice, but I wasn't sure anyone wanted to hear what I had to say. Some said, "Start blogging." I looked up the word *blog*, wrote a few, and fell in love with the interaction and access in today's world.

The more I spoke, the more I realized that anyone who did think he or she knew me defined me as that rich woman with the gift-wrapping room. I was the mother who may or may not have given her children all the money they thought they deserved, the quiet woman on the arm of one of Hollywood's most powerful executives, and another one of the wives of Hollywood with the beautiful clothes at the star-studded parties.

Exposing my opinions means exposing myself. It has been scary, but enlightening, threatening, and exhilarating, and I'm having fun.

When I was offered the opportunity to write a book with stories about my life, I instantly said yes. I was ready.

I've always loved telling stories. As a shy child and, later, as a wife not encouraged to speak, I often created stories about my surroundings, people I'd see, places I wanted to go. I'd look at characters in paintings or figures in statues and imagine what they were thinking or what they'd do next. I'd imagine how much fun my friends were having on dates, or how happy Tori and Randy must be at school with their friends and favorite teachers while I was cooking their dinner at home.

This book relates many of the stories of my life and the stories I've imagined about how life can be.

I've been on a wonderful ride, exposed to some of the most interesting people and places in the world, while struggling with the issues of my baby boomer generation as we moved from innocent children to conflicted teens, through marriage, motherhood.

Things might have been a lot different if my parents had encouraged me to write rather than fold napkins. I remember two letters I did write as a child. One was to my father, apologizing if my cooking had caused him to have an ulcer. My parents thought it was adorable and gave it to the local newspaper to publish.

And I wrote a will when I was nine.

My family was eating dinner, and half a worm emerged from my artichoke. Convinced that I had just eaten the other half, I screamed and announced I was probably going to die. Neat and organized from an early age, I decided I had to write "my will" and say goodbye to my family. I found out years later that my mother kept it. She could at least have corrected the spelling and punctuation for me.

MY WILL

When I die from eating a worm I leave all my poseshons to my family, Mom, Pop & Brother & Morgen.

To My Mom, I will leave ⅓ of my astate & to My Pop I leave ⅓ of my astate & to my brother I leave ⅓ of my astate, which is $30.00, and also I leave my dog Morgen to my Mom and Morgen will get the rest of my poseshons, which whatever they may be.

Signature / Candy Marer

1954

Fortunately, I did not die. Morgan was my stuffed animal and best friend, and I remember being worried that my mom might not take as good care of him as I did.

Anyway, looking back, I see that my writing, spelling, and punctuation could have used some help, but my business acumen was clearly in place.

My mother and I never talked about it, and I hadn't thought about that will for years until Aaron mentioned it years after we got married.

I couldn't imagine how he could know the story of my will, even though, by that time, he was working on *The Mod Squad* and had produced detective shows such as *Honey West* and *Burke's Law*. He'd uncovered the evidence just as easily as his TV characters did.

With a flourish as suave as Amos Burke's, he showed me that my mother had given him my will. He handed me my note, attached to a letter, written in her beautiful handwriting on Beverly Hillcrest Hotel stationery, which read:

My Darling Aaron,
Please take good care of this for me, as I'd die if it ever got lost. It's one of my fondest memories of Candy—before she married you and got smart & learned to spell.
I love you,
"Mom"

It was nice to hear that my mother thought I'd "got smart," but I never did learn to spell very well. Aaron, of course, was a great speller.

I've been fortunate to have people looking out for me. Now I'm enjoying starting to realize what is actually right for me.

I've sure had an interesting time living my *Stories from Candyland*. I'm glad you're coming along to read them.

Stories from Candyland

Chapter 1

My Rock for the Ages

I loved Fridays. Instead of taking the school bus home, I'd go in the opposite direction and run to the big newsstand where all my favorite movie magazines were sold. I could barely contain myself until I'd seen the black truck full of afternoon newspapers and weekly magazines approach, heard the thud of the heavy stacks of magazines hitting the sidewalk.

I was always hungry on Fridays because I had long ago

decided that my money was better spent on magazines than on another elementary school lunch. Nevertheless, I had the strength to move aside the magazines about cars and food and sports until the movie star covers appeared.

One special Friday I ran into my house hugging two full-color, star-studded magazines of celebrity secrets to my chest. I found my mother in the kitchen and announced, "Mom, I might be late for dinner. I have a lot of reading to do."

"Candy, you're never going to have any money if you spend it all on those movie star magazines."

That's what my mother told me constantly. This was the same mother who had named me "Carole Gene," after Carole Lombard, a movie star my mother loved when she read about her years earlier in the same movie star magazines.

Carole Lombard was an okay star, and no one called me "Carole" anyway. I was Candy, and I was in love with Rock Hudson. I knew it from a young age, when the twenty cents that copies of *Photoplay* and *Modern Screen* cost far exceeded my allowance. Thank goodness for birthdays, holidays, and teeth falling out, which were all good for a few more cents.

Rock's photo was on the cover of the February 1957 issue of *Photoplay*. "Rock Hudson's Life Story," the headline promised. I devoured every word. I discounted the photos of Rock with his wife. In the August 1954 issue of *Modern Screen*, the cover had asked the question "Is Rock Hudson Afraid of Marriage?" If he was afraid in 1954, why was he married? Hmm. Maybe the marriage wouldn't last. One of my friends' parents were getting divorced, and Rock and his wife didn't have kids.

I found out that his name was originally Roy Scherer. I didn't know anyone named Rock or Roy, but that would change someday. I knew he would be mine in just a few years, as soon as I grew up. One day I discovered there was even a food named for the two of us, a clear sign we were meant to be together. I found a recipe for rock candy, and learned how to make it in different colors. Rock and I would eat it every night for dessert to celebrate our love.

I learned that Rock might be afraid of marriage around the time I saw the ad for his new movie, *Magnificent Obsession*. I had no idea what the title meant, but I read and reread the words in the ad: "This was the moment unashamed . . . when this man and this woman felt the first ecstasy of their Magnificent Obsession." No clue. Good photo, though. My parents wouldn't let me see the movie. Now I own it on DVD.

Screen Album magazine wrote in the summer of 1956, "Tall, handsome, in demand as an escort, Rock Hudson played, and committed himself to no one. I'll marry when I'm 30 said he—and who, in his position, would have rushed? The world can be fun for a man with no ties, and a pocketful of green money." Wait, Rock. Wait until you're closer to forty, so I have time to grow up. I'm growing as fast as I can. I'm not sure why you're married now, but don't get married again until you're forty and ready for me. Okay?

The stories sent me on a roller-coaster fantasy life. My copy of the "Big Spring Issue—Who Loves Who in Hollywood!" of *Motion Picture* magazine in 1956 named the couples who were most in love: Debbie Reynolds and Eddie Fisher, Liz Taylor and Michael Wilding, Janet Leigh and Tony Curtis, and (sigh) Rock Hudson and Phyllis Gates. Something was fishy. I had recently seen photos of "Rock and Liz in Texas" in *Silver Screen*. He didn't look like he was thinking of anyone named Phyllis, and there didn't seem to be a Michael on *her* mind.

Then again, maybe his marriage wouldn't last. *Motion Picture* described the wedding day: "He was dressed in a brown suit and he looked wonderful, so handsome. Phyllis, warm, friendly, curly-haired, did him the honor as his wife." I knew that's what a wife should do. I didn't like that magazine because it wrote about Rock's wife, and I vowed not to buy it again, even though it was cheaper than the others, at fifteen cents.

Stop the presses. My *Photoplay* in May 1957 was all about the "Todd-Taylor Marriage." More hope. Maybe Mr. Wilding would take the honorable Mrs. Gates Hudson away from my Rock. There was hope again.

My collection of Rock Hudson stories and photos grew. I had seen *Pillow Talk* about twelve times (I had a bigger allowance), as I kept growing closer to Rock's age. I knew I had it made in 1962 when *Motion Picture* ("first and best" and twenty-five cents) wrote about Rock's "reflections." He was so deep and dreamy.

Asked what he admired about Jackie Kennedy, Rock said,

"I think she has beautiful hairdos." Guess what! I had a Jackie Kennedy hairdo, although my hair was blond and fine. Oh, Rock! The writer asked what he liked most about Doris Day. "I like her humor, her sunniness." Rock, people tell me I look like Doris Day, and I have a good sense of humor. Perfect! But my mother insisted there was no such word as *sunniness*.

By the middle 1960s, I was ready to get together with Rock. Yes, I'd dated a lot of boys at school, gotten married at seventeen and divorced at nineteen, and dated again, but I would have dropped everything now that I was old enough to marry Rock Hudson. Sometimes, when I was out to dinner, or in a Beverly Hills department store, people would say, "Rock Hudson was here just last week." Bad timing for me, but I was still optimistic.

⚜

In 1966 I started dating a man named Aaron Spelling. He made me nervous because he had quite a reputation as a playboy. Even though I was twenty, I knew I was no match for a sophisticated and worldly playboy. I agreed to a date, we enjoyed ourselves, and I accepted a second date. I liked him a lot, even though his playboy image, social ease, and maturity scared me.

"Candy," Aaron's voice crackled from the massive car phone that took up half his front seat, "I've been invited to a party for Grace Kelly on Saturday night. We can go there on our date."

A party for Grace Kelly? Oh my. Grace Kelly was the most beautiful, most elegant woman alive. I think that if she had been a star when I was born, my mother might have named me "Grace Gene."

I was so excited that I missed Aaron's next sentence: "The party is at Rock Hudson's house in Hollywood. Candy, do you want to go to Rock's for Grace Kelly's party?"

"What rocks?" I said.

"I told you. The party is at Rock Hudson's house."

The world stopped. Everything started spinning. I was afraid my heart was going to fly right out of my chest. I was going to Rock Hudson's house!

The next four days seemed to take four years. I shopped for clothes I couldn't afford, and looked through every fashion magazine over and over to find the right hairstyle and makeup look for the evening. I also called all the people who had ever made fun of me for having a magnificent obsession with Rock Hudson. Carole Gene Marer was going to Rock Hudson's house.

By the time Aaron picked me up in his black Cadillac Eldorado Brougham, I was giddy. I'm a very shy person and don't talk much, but Aaron couldn't shut me up. In retrospect, I think I sounded like Alvin and his chipmunk friends, chatting incessantly.

We arrived at a white house surrounded by beautiful flowers at the top of a hill in Hollywood. I started shaking. Were we having an earthquake? Oh no. Not tonight. Please.

It wasn't an earthquake. It was my nerves.

We walked in, and every one of the stars whose photos and lives I had studied and admired in my movie magazines appeared before my eyes. Someone snapped our picture. And then, suddenly, there he was. Rock Hudson! He was tall, dark, and handsome, just like the magazines said he was. He was smiling. Wait. He was smiling at Aaron and me. He was walking toward us. Rock Hudson was just feet away from my feet.

Then my feet took me to Rock Hudson's bathroom, and that's where I stayed the entire night. I was so nervous, so scared, so overwhelmed—so of course the answer was to lock myself in Rock Hudson's bathroom and hope no one would need to use it.

I remember all three of the sentences I said to guests at that party that evening. "It's occupied. You can't come in. Go away." Anyone who tried the door, knocked, stomped, or asked if anyone was in there got one or all of my three phrases.

I also remember what people were saying. Many of the voices were familiar. I found out that celebrities talk about their kids, the weather, vacations, cars, clothes, and all the other things normal adults do.

Aaron's voice was always in the distance. He had this Texas accent that gave him a very distinctive sound. He's a playboy. He'll find someone else to hang around with to-night, I remember thinking. He won't even miss me.

I'm not sure how long I was locked in the bathroom, but soon I was jolted by the realization that the person knocking on the door was my date, Aaron.

"Candy. Is that you in there? Are you sick? What's the matter? We have to leave. The party is ending. Candy?"

I froze right there on the toilet seat in Rock Hudson's bathroom. I had been discovered. I hadn't really thought this through. I hadn't realized I'd have to leave the bathroom eventually.

Okay. I had taken ballroom dancing lessons, gone to etiquette class, studied movie star habits, and had very polite relatives, so I could do this right.

I casually strolled out of the bathroom, took Aaron's hand, and we walked quickly out the front door.

"What in the world happened? Why were you in the bathroom all night?"

"Aaron, I was so scared. You know how shy I am. I've wanted to meet Rock Hudson all my life. And when it was time, I knew I'd have nothing to say or I'd sound stupid, and that I shouldn't be with those kinds of people, and I just ended up in the bathroom."

Aaron took my hand and laughed. And laughed.

I remember thinking that this suave, popular playboy wouldn't be asking Candy the social misfit out again.

I was wrong. We had a third date, although it was very unconventional. Aaron spent our entire third date tutoring me. We worked on looking at each other right in the eye. We shook each other's hands over and over. We practiced small talk. He trained me for future dates. He said I had passed. We had a fourth date, a fifth, sixth . . .

We didn't go to a lot of Hollywood parties on the next few dates. We went to the Cocoanut Grove nightclub and heard dreamy Eddie Fisher sing. We went backstage after the show, and I played with his puppy while he and Aaron spoke. We would go the popular local clubs, the Daisy, the Factory, or the Candy Store. Aaron was a great dancer, and I wasn't too shy about my dancing. None of our succeeding dates involved Rock Hudson.

I did finally get to meet Grace Kelly many times in later years. But better still, Rock and I became great friends, and he even later appeared in Aaron's series *Dynasty*. I don't know if he ever remembered that I was the perfectly coiffed young woman who had occupied his bathroom for hours. He was such a nice man. If he did remember, he would probably have been too polite to mention it. I liked thinking that he didn't know it was me.

Aaron and I had a very happy marriage for thirty-eight years. We loved the time we spent laughing with Rock and his friends. I never told Rock any of my stories about my infatuation for him and my plans for when I grew up. I probably would have locked myself in the bathroom in embarrassment if he had ever found out.

But I have kept many of the magazine stories about him all these years.

Chapter 2

❋

Dr. Spock or Mr. Spock: Did We Really Listen to These Guys?

I've lost count of how many e-mails I've received about how we baby boomers grew up to be such independent people because we rode our bikes without helmets, were herded into cars without seat belts, car seats, or air bags, lived in homes painted in pretty lead-based colors, filled up on white bread and butter, drank tap water, got Band-Aids instead of trips to the emergency room for cuts and scrapes, played outdoors after dark, and engaged in all kinds of now-primitive-sounding activities. The punch line is that, by today's standards, it's a miracle we survived.

I think we had more fun. We had more freedom, were encouraged to be creative and less structured, and learned those good old values and work ethics. (No, I'm not running for office.)

And all this despite all the parenting experts who, like us, were breathing lead-based paint fumes and risking their lives in station wagons and on scooters.

I wonder how many more virtues we could give ourselves if we and our parents hadn't spent so much time listening to people like Dr. Spock and Mr. Spock.

Sometimes, when I try to figure out what my mother was thinking during her child-rearing years, I remember the copy of *Dr. Spock's Baby and Child Care* that never seemed to be too far out of her reach.

My mother wasn't the only Spock devotee. I recognized his child care manual at all my friends' houses, too. The book was published the year I was born, and I bought the updated versions of the "timeless bestseller" when Tori and Randy were born. I wanted to be as knowledgeable as the mothers before me.

I don't think Dr. Spock helped my mother or me very much.

In between advice and thoughts on everything from diaper use to proper diet, from crying to reading, from the limits of love to raising children in a troubled society, from colic to body development, Dr. Spock wrote:

> In many ways, we have lost our faith in the meaning of life and our confidence to understand our world and our society. My point here is that you are raising your children in the context of very confusing and rapidly changing times. Your goals and aspirations for your child are going to be greatly influenced by these times and the prevailing ideals and beliefs.

That's not a very positive message. Then I discovered more of his uplifting words:

> Parenting is an ideal guilt-generating business, and labor often delivers the first volley. . . . The "perfect" parent has yet to see the light of day.

All right. That explains some of my mother's attitudes, I guess.

By the time my kids were born, I had two Spocks to consult. Dr. Spock kept updating his book, and Mr. Spock of *Star Trek* was among pop culture's most quoted figures. If Dr. Spock was right about the times influencing our beliefs as they related to child-rearing, I thought I might as well use the other Spock to check in on what people were thinking and believing. Most people I knew in the 1970s didn't know

that Dr. Spock and Mr. Spock weren't the same person anyway. Both pontificated.

Mr. Spock's deep thoughts included:

If there are self-made purgatories, then we all have to live
in them. Mine can be no worse than someone else's.

It is curious how often you humans manage to obtain that
which you do not want.

I am endeavoring, ma'am, to construct a mnemonic circuit
using stone knives and bearskins.

Nowhere am I so desperately needed as among a shipload
of illogical humans.

I really couldn't relate to either of the Spocks. So I decided to investigate what other resources my mother had
when my brother and I were growing up.

I remember my first book of *Nursery Rhymes* (which I
still have) and my mother reading:

> *Little Polly Flinders sat among the cinders,*
> *Warming her pretty little toes!*

Mother would pause here to tell me I had pretty little
toes, too.

Dr. Spock or Mr. Spock

Her mother came and caught her,
And whipped her little daughter,
For spoiling her nice new clothes.

Lesson learned. I never sat in cinders and spoiled nice new clothes.

The *Reader's Digest* from my birth month featured "So You Think You've Got Rationing Troubles," and warned of "butter-berserk housewives," "soprano voices demanding beef," and "improvident housewives."

My mother was none of the above, but she collected multiples of everything, and encouraged me to do the same. I don't remember my parents ever running out of anything. I bought my kids two of everything "just in case." I think I still have some of those obsolete toys and long-out-of-fashion clothes in my attic.

Another *Reader's Digest* story challenged parents to adopt the new post–World War II role of the United States in the "community of nations" with "service and leadership." My family was the first on our block to have a fully stocked bomb shelter in the 1950s. I guess that made us leaders.

One of my mother's favorite magazines was *Country Gentleman*, even though she was a native of Los Angeles and a lady. The advice the month I was born was, "Don't raise hogs for pets." We only had one dog—briefly—and never did get a hog.

Her issue of *The Woman* magazine had a sad story: "My

Sons Had Polio." Whenever I complained about anything, from eating peas to too much homework, my mother would say, "At least you don't have polio." She was right. I was very lucky.

The *Life* magazine that was on the stands when I was born (with a victorious General Douglas MacArthur on the cover) provided much parenting and life advice.

If my mother brushed my teeth with Ipana, I would never have "pink toothbrush." (I think I always had pretty pink toothbrushes in my bathroom.) She shampooed my hair with Kreml shampoo, the only shampoo used by "Lovely Powers Models" (and she later encouraged me to become a lovely John Robert Powers model myself). She kept a bottle of the drug *Atropa belladonna* handy in case I developed "deadly nightshade" or anything else that could be cured by the drug that "relieves much human suffering."

Her magazines helped educate me, too. The importance of the alphabet was stressed in ads for her favorite cigarette. "Your ABC for more smoking pleasure," the ad in *Life* told her.

Let the first three letters of the alphabet remind you why Chesterfield gives you all the benefits of smoking pleasure . . . Always Buy Chesterfield . . . Always milder; Better tasting; Cooler smoking." ABCDEFG . . . HIJK-LMNO-Puff that cigarette.

Dr. Spock or Mr. Spock

I guess my mother was a student of the culture, and that's how she brought me up.

Good Housekeeping had a story the month I was born that said that trade schools would be the wave of the future. Boys would become engineers. Girls would learn advanced sewing and cooking, and the best of the best would graduate from sewing to working in big, important stores. I succeeded. I got a job at Joseph Magnin and worked my way up from salesgirl in Casual (cheap) Dresses to manager of the Lingerie Department.

I was prepared for a career in retail. My parents took me out of public school for a while and sent me to a too-expensive (my father said) private school, where I learned how to be the proper young lady. I curtsied, spoke in the right tone, danced beautifully, could set a table, and missed two years of spelling. My friend Nancy, who went to the same school, misspells many of the same words I do. It has been our private shame, except now it's being made public, in my book. *Sorry, Nancy. I'de like you're forgivness.*

I tried to be like my mother. She was beautiful. I'd try on her wigs and hold her cigarette the way she did, to look chic. She said I looked silly.

We had lots of rules in our house, and I was expected to follow them all. Her wish for me was that I marry a successful man, so I wouldn't have to struggle the way she had.

"You'll never marry a rich man if you don't listen to me,"

she would say, as she told me I was too shy, that I slouched, that my hair wasn't right, or that she didn't like the expression on my face.

I was terrified of making a mistake. My shyness intensified. I didn't want to say the wrong thing or make an inappropriate move. I thought that if I looked down, people wouldn't notice me. I was never sure what I was supposed to do. Half the time, I was sent away from the dinner table, and I was rarely told the reason. But I did know I was being "trained."

The biggest pressure, though, was that I was commanded to be "perfect." My brother was imperfect, my parents decided (as did his teachers and the parents of his friends), so I had to make up for his behavior. I tried hard. But perfection and I never bonded.

Mothers want the best for their daughters, and mine was no exception. She wanted to be a decorator, so she was glad when I became interested in interior design. I think she even approved when I went to art college. She and I would sit side by side sewing, and I still have throughout my home some of the beautiful cushions and covers we created together.

My mother's family had been very poor. Ours had its ups and downs, changing lifestyles on short notice. My father was a traveling salesman. When he came home, we were never sure if we were going to have to move again or stay in our current house. My shyness intensified every time we moved. I knew my mother felt bad about this. She didn't want that kind of insecurity for her Candy.

I don't think my mother ever got all the way through Dr. Spock's book. If she did, she must have decided that she didn't like a lot of what it said.

I came to the same conclusion.

By the time Tori was born, in 1973, and Randy in 1978, my husband had achieved tremendous success. Although I didn't fulfill my mother's dream of marrying a rich man, the man I married did become rich during our marriage.

By then I could afford nannies and nurses and all the child care experts in the world for my kids; but Aaron and I were very hands-on parents. We tried so hard to be perfect parents, but found there's no such thing.

Hmm. Maybe Dr. Spock was right after all. He said the "perfect parent had yet to see the light of day."

I have, literally, thousands of photographs throughout my house of Tori and Randy at every stage of their lives: playing, running, eating; at holiday and family gatherings; on their first day of school, last day of school; with their first bike, first car; playing with the dogs, in the pool, on vacation. Every moment was a joy, every minute a learning experience—and every day we lived in fear that we were doing something wrong.

We loved staying home and being with our kids, couldn't wait to share the next life experience with them, and Aaron and I were always much happier at the kitchen table with the kids than at the best table at the most "in" restaurant.

We raised really good kids. I complain about my mother.

My daughter complains about me. The culture has evolved. Now a million people a week hear Tori's ever-evolving memories of her childhood on her TV show. In retrospect, she seems to think our good times weren't as good as others remember them. I think they were.

Tori related a story in her book about the great times we had on the beach and the joy we shared when she found beautiful seashells. Also in her book, however, she recounts how she now resents that I scattered some of the shells on the beach just so she could find them.

A few years ago, when my husband was writing his own book, Tori had a different memory.

Aaron wrote in his autobiography, *A Prime-Time Life*:

I'll let Tori tell you some of her favorite memories about growing up:

> . . . in Malibu, at our beach house, Mom and Dad used to take us walking on the beach all the time, and they'd have Randy and me search for seashells. Somehow we always found these beautiful seashells, the kind they sell for five dollars and up in coastal souvenir shops. I didn't find out until later that Mom and Dad had the seashells buried for us.

It was one of Aaron's and my "favorite memories," too. With apologies to Mr. Spock, Tori, we were not endeavoring, ma'am, to construct a mnemonic circuit using stone knives and bearskins. We were trying to construct for our children the best lives in the world. And, in retrospect, that's what my parents were trying to do for me, too.

Maybe Dr. Spock's next version will provide a roadmap for all of us. I'll never stop trying to be the perfect mom.

Chapter 3

⚜

Fred Astaire Asked Me to Dance Because I'se Biggest

I was married to one of the great storytellers of all time. I didn't have to say a word. I lived a storied life, and everyone thought they knew my life story. They didn't. That was all right. His stories were fun, exciting, and larger than life.

My late husband, Aaron Spelling, rewrote pop culture with his shows. *The Mod Squad* and *Dynasty* dictated fashion trends. (Nolan Miller's fashions from *Dynasty* became instantly recognizable.) It was all about the hair in *Charlie's*

Angels. *Fantasy Island* and *The Love Boat* are still synonyms for vacations. Who doesn't know where *90210* is or who lives there? *Melrose Place* started showing up on tourist maps. His movie *Mr. Mom* redefined spousal roles. Everyone wanted a *Starsky & Hutch* car. The "fight" between Linda Evans and Joan Collins, dragging each other around in the water, became instant camp; and we laughed when we heard stories about how fans were re-creating the scene at parties.

Everyone knew Aaron's stories and those of the characters on his shows. When we went out, I had to be the best-dressed perfect wife, the ultimate model of the Hollywood wife, one who appeared to have stepped right out of one of Aaron's shows. It was a role I accepted gladly. I wanted to please Aaron and be the wife such a successful man should have. We both had our jobs and knew other people's expectations. But given a choice of attending a Hollywood gala or being home with the kids, we would always choose to stay home.

While Aaron was creating his television and movie stories, I was at home in my jeans, T-shirts, and sweats creating plots of my own.

And then there's my humming. I hum all the time. When I think, I hum. I might ponder what I'm going to say in a meeting, so I hum as I'm walking toward the office.

I hum songs such as "Oh, What a Beautiful Morning" when I think about how great the day can be, or "You Make Me Feel So Young" if my story doesn't fit with my age.

My humming causes other people to make up stories, too.

When I hum as I walk into a store or restaurant, someone usually says, "Oh, you're happy today."

Tori didn't like my humming. We were at her school buying her uniforms once and she announced that I was a major embarrassment to her. "Do you have to hum?" Probably. I hadn't thought about it. I felt bad about embarrassing her.

I hum when I'm deep in thought. And I hum when I'm nervous. The night before my first-ever appearance on QVC with my Candy Spelling dolls, I knew I was nervous when I went to bed. I never imagined that I would hum so loudly I'd wake myself up! But I did.

I could never sneak up on Aaron or the kids. They would hear me coming by my humming. "You'd make a terrible spy," Aaron used to say. I didn't want to be a spy. I just loved humming.

I've always loved stories. In fact, I have a story about just about everything in my house, and that's a lot of stories.

My favorite painting hangs just outside the library, where all of Aaron's scripts are kept. I saw it in an auction catalog and was determined to get it for our home. It is called *I'se Biggest*, and it was painted in 1892 by British artist Arthur Elsley. It's a scene of an adorable smiling little girl—all dressed up in her Sunday best—standing next to her Saint Bernard to measure her height. She's standing on books and on her tiptoes, trying to be as tall as she can be.

I can tell from the delight on the little girl's face that, for the first time, she feels "biggest." I identify with that little girl. I've spent my life trying to measure myself and get bigger, biggest. The little girl in the painting isn't bigger than her dog, who is lovingly and protectively looking at her. That doesn't stop her from believing "I'se biggest." She's happy, and I share in her happiness.

Her attitude is one I've always wanted. "I can do anything I want," I'd imagine her saying. Then I'd imagine winning an Olympic medal, being perfect, or becoming the first woman president, even though I didn't really want any of those. I just wanted to feel like I could.

I have a collection of hand-painted fans that I keep in a delicate cabinet adjacent to my bedroom. I have to refrain from handling them when I visit them daily because they are so fragile, but that doesn't stop me from creating stories about each one. Each fan is so special. Some have actual ivory on their tiny surfaces; others have the most subtle gold leafing; and mother-of-pearl casually adorns a couple of the paper fans. I can't imagine how anyone had the patience or steadiness to hand-stitch those perfect borders. I couldn't do it. They amaze and delight me.

I try to imagine who painted each one, wonder what he or she looked like, the shape and size of the room in which the artist worked, how much in love he or she might have been to be able to paint the most romantic scenes, how many people before me owned the fans, in what kinds of beautiful houses they were kept.

I fell in love with fans on a trip to France in 1989. My

mood was romantic then, so I began buying fans with romantic scenes.

One of my first fans has a boy on one side, and he's carrying what I've decided is a love letter. On the other end is a little girl and her dog. Even though the fan is only two inches tall, the boy and girl will never get to reach each other; but the anticipation and joy in their faces is enough to assure me how happy they will be for eternity.

I have another fan that was painted in France in 1914. It shows an elegant couple dancing. The dancers look like Fred Astaire and Ginger Rogers to me, dancing in *Top Hat*, *Shall We Dance*, and *The Gay Divorcee*, those romantic movies they made in the 1930s. I look at the fan and hear "Night and Day," "Let's Face the Music," and "Lovely to Look At," and I hear Fred Astaire singing those songs to me.

More than once, that little fan has inspired me to dance around the room, imagining that Fred chose me over Ginger. I worry I'll lose count . . . *one, two, three, and one, two, three, and one, two, three*. Is that the polka with Yul Brynner in *The King and I* or Astaire's Carioca in *Flying Down to Rio*? It doesn't matter. Fred chose me over Ginger, and we're dancing cheek to cheek; Fred holding me tight, looking into my eyes, just like the couple on my fan.

One very racy fan shows a couple on a swing, and they're kissing. On the other side of this fan is a beautiful bouquet of flowers. I'm convinced he's just proposed to her, and they are kissing to celebrate. The flowers will be part of her bridal bou-quiet. After the wedding, they'll return to the swing, and then kiss on the swing on their anniversary, and then bring their children (a girl and a boy) to the swing with them. What could be more romantic, and who is going to dispute my story?

After a while, I started buying fans with clowns on them. I'm not sure why, except that I like laughing just a little less than I love romance.

I can't help smiling when I look at my fans and the silly but regal-looking clowns who smile back at me. None of them looks like a Bozo or Chuckles. One in particular has a girl clown on one end and a boy on the other, who I've imagined are about to meet, fall in love, redefine romance, conquer the clown industry, and then be invited to entertain British royalty. I'm waiting to read that the beautiful clown couple has joined superstars such as Sir Paul McCartney and Sir Elton John as knights.

I have stories about my Steuben figures, too. Those figurines bring out some of my best obsessive-compulsive behavior. I know where each piece belongs, if "he" or "she" has been moved, and who belongs with whom.

I have a family of three Steuben beavers. Leave it to Candy.

My husband gave me the most beautiful Steuben hearts for my birthdays, Mother's Day, and other special occasions. One has the key to his heart. I keep all the hearts together, and remember how much I loved Aaron. And, of course, I make up romantic stories about where some of the Steubens lived before they reached my home, the romantic thoughts the other owners had as they admired the pieces, the secrets the pieces might have overheard in other people's houses, and even some of the travel adventures they might have had. I have no worries that any of them would ever be inclined to tip off the tabloids about any of the exploits they've witnessed.

When Aaron and I got married in 1968, my mother gave me a beautiful Steuben bowl. My wonderful husband bought me crystal fruit to fill it. He's the only man I ever knew who could make apples, plums, bananas, grapes, and pears romantic.

I think my Steuben mushrooms are right out of *Alice's Adventures in Wonderland*, and that delights me.

I imagine that my dog, Madison, hangs out with some of my Steuben animals when I'm not home. She can play, but she'd better not touch. I wonder if she likes the giraffes or elephants more. Does she discriminate? No, Madison loves almost everyone.

Although most of my stories are happy fantasies and great memories, one piece of art serves a valuable purpose.

Directly across from "the Mrs. chair" in my office is a painting called *Lily Garden*, by Louis Ritman. It's a beautiful painting filled with colorful and blooming flowers, and a woman at work faced with two paths winding through the purples, greens, and reds of the gardens. When my work gets overwhelming—and that kind of stress hits me maybe fifteen or twenty times a day—I imagine myself strolling on one of those two paths to another place.

I always have work to do, and whenever there's a crisis

with one of my charities or an emergency city commission meeting, or if there's a problem with one of my kids or grandchildren, I snap into action. But I have a secret weapon. I gaze at those peaceful paths across the room. I imagine myself as idle as the woman in the painting, walking down one of those paths to nowhere and everywhere, as carefree as the flowers enjoying the spring breeze.

I'm even able to cope when I hear a story about how Tori announced on her TV show that I didn't attend a lavish party she threw. I want to yell to the tourists in the buses parked outside my house, "But I wasn't invited!" but instead I imagine myself on one of those idyllic paths. I fantasize about finding a handwritten note from Tori among the lilies. It reads, "Dear Mom: Come on over . . . anytime. Bring Randy. Love, Tori." I can't wait to call my son, Randy, to tell him the good news. There's no cell phone on these paths, so I'll call him as soon as I finish my walk down the path to happiness. He'll be happy, too.

Aaron told stories about families, romance, relationships, law and order, good and bad, fantasies and faith. For decades, millions of people tuned in every week to hear those stories and see how they related to their own.

My stories have an audience of just one, but I have a lot less pressure. No network executives can change my words. No sponsors can say I'm being too bold. My characters don't have egos or rules. And if my audience of one doesn't like the way the plot is going, I can change it. That's a plot I like.

Chapter 4

Hollywood Wife and Mother 101: A Star Isn't Born

I always had mixed feelings about being the spouse of a famous person.

I felt so sorry for Norman Maine in *A Star Is Born*, his frustrations and problems increasing as his wife's star rose.

I often wondered what Mrs. Spencer Tracy was thinking at premieres when Tracy and Katharine Hepburn were exchanging loving glances.

On the other hand, I'd see the wives of big stars such as

Clark Gable and Rock Hudson and think they must have great lives. They could be shy women like I was, yet get to go to all the best events, wear the most gorgeous clothes, and meet exciting people.

I really didn't expect to become the wife of a famous man, so I never decided if there were more pros or cons involved. And then I became one.

When I met Aaron Spelling in 1966, he was more famous as a Hollywood playboy than as a Hollywood executive. He was the life of the party, a great date, a laugh a minute. And I wanted no part of him. I was looking for solid and successful, not Hollywood stereotypical.

We dated on and off for the next two and a half years. I moved to New York to get away from him. I returned, we got a marriage license, and it expired. I moved to San Francisco. I always came back. He had enlisted my parents' help.

Love prevailed, though, and we did get married. After all that time, we thought about driving to Las Vegas to do so, but my parents had been Aaron's secret allies to persuade me to marry him, and he wanted them to be there. So we got married at their apartment in West Hollywood; my mother and father; my brother, Tony; Aaron's brother, Danny; and a close family friend were there with us. That night my parents hosted a beautiful reception for about forty friends in the rec room of their building. It was wonderful, and I still look at our wedding pictures all the time to remember that happy day.

My new husband was smart, charming, and in debt, owing

money on a house he had had to give his ex-wife, actress Carolyn Jones. He had some good Hollywood credits to his name, but was a staff writer or producer then, and never envisioned or dreamed of anything that would become an "Aaron Spelling Production." Besides, he had always wanted to be an actor, but small roles on *I Love Lucy*, *Gunsmoke*, *Dragnet*, and *Alfred Hitchcock Presents* wouldn't pay many bills. Still, he was an incredibly smart and talented man who, like many others, was looking for his big break in show business.

It's not news at this point that my husband became one of the most successful, and thus famous, producers in Hollywood history. His list of credits causes people to gasp first and then nod and smile, and almost everyone has a story about how one of the episodes from *The Mod Squad*, *Fantasy Island*, or *Beverly Hills 90210* impacted his or her life.

Aaron's success provided us with a life of luxury almost beyond imagination. And, yes, we were invited to every great party, got to meet many of the most interesting people in the world, and enjoyed experiences that were better than those of a lot of his television characters.

But we were just a regular couple who wanted children—although I wanted children much more than he did. But I was not able to get pregnant. We tried everything. The more I couldn't get pregnant, the more I wanted a baby. I became obsessed with taking my temperature, so we wouldn't miss an opportunity. I made Aaron come home from the office for yet another attempt, and repeated the steps over and over.

Finally, when it looked like I couldn't get pregnant, Aaron agreed that we would adopt a baby.

Once the pressure was off, even before we started applying to adopt a baby, I got pregnant. We were blessed with Tori in 1973, and after much trying, Randy was born prematurely more than five and a half years later, in 1978, when I was just six and a half months into the pregnancy.

I had always loved the name Victoria, and dreamed of having a daughter I could give that name. But in true Candy style, I worried that her nickname would become "Vicki," and I didn't want that. We named our daughter Victoria, but at the suggestion of her godmother, Barbara Stanwyck, we called her Tori immediately. Barbara said, "Why don't you nickname her Tori before the kids decide on another name?"

The ultimate irony was that Tori was conceived during the annual television "pilot" season, a time when producers such as Aaron, already working twenty-hour days, were putting in even more hours. He was never as pressured as during pilot season, and 1972, when he was working on getting *The Rookies* on the air, was no exception. The timing of my pregnancy might have made a great episode for one of his fantasy shows.

Over the years, I had learned a lot of lessons about the pitfalls of being a Hollywood stage mother, and Aaron and I were determined that our kids would be as "normal" as the circumstances permitted. It's difficult to explain to children that there's nothing special about them when you go to the movies as a family and photographers yell, "Candy, Tori,

Randy, Aaron! Over here! Smile," or when strangers ask them for their autographs before they've even learned how to write their names. We were offered the best tables at restaurants, despite lines of people waiting, and the kids were often told they were "beautiful," "handsome," and/or "smart" by complete strangers, who'd stare at and examine them thoroughly. It was heady stuff, especially for the kids.

We were lucky, though, in that Aaron and I were basically homebodies, and dinner at home with the kids was the ultimate pleasure for us. Our kids had privileges, but they did have rules, too. The trick was to balance the two.

When Tori was very young, she started talking about becoming an actress. Oh no, I thought. I don't want her to become one of those "child stars," and I'm not going to become one of those terrible mothers pulling her kid out of school for auditions, rejections, singing lessons, meetings, and other activities that had no place in a normal child's life.

I had seen so much heartache with actors and actresses, and I didn't want my little girl to become part of what could be the most insecure and unreliable profession, where failures were magnified and so public. I thought it would be nice to expose her to different kinds of experiences; and when she was older, if she still decided she wanted to act, I wouldn't try to stop her.

But Tori was persistent. My husband was madly in love with his little girl and couldn't stop himself from casting her to get her established. That's a short way of telling you what you already know: Tori became an actress. She earned millions of dollars on her father's show *Beverly Hills 90210*, where she appeared in 292 episodes; and she had other high-paying acting and producing jobs, as well. She benefited far more than most actors, as her father even arranged for her to be represented by the top Hollywood talent agency.

The kids' early visits to the sets were a combination of Disneyland and seeing Dad at work. The pilot for *Charlie's Angels* had been shot at our house on North Mapleton Drive (just blocks from where my present home, The Manor, would later be built), so the kids were used to all the cameras, crew, and chaos. Randy would get excited examining everything, and Tori loved the glamour of it all.

I remember Tori begging her father to let her "act" when she was four. I didn't encourage it, because I knew the life of rejection most actresses led. Her first role was on his series *Vega$,* where she had a recurring role as the daughter of Bea, Dan Tana's secretary.

Her first line, which we rehearsed for what seemed like hours, was, "Hi, Uncle Dan." She nailed it in one take, and her father couldn't have been prouder.

Randy first appeared as "Ryan," the younger half brother of Ian Ziering's character on *Beverly Hills 90210*. He was billed as "little blond boy," and he helped out at the beach club. He and Tori were in different scenes, and he would get caught up in her excitement, too.

We were both very proud of her. She was a millionaire mini-mogul, acting and getting ready to produce, wanting to follow in her father's footsteps. She worked hard, had a thick skin when it came to accusations of nepotism, and she did quite well.

Randy was more casual about his acting than his sister was. It was more about fun than passion for him.

As both got older, I knew I couldn't control their career choices. And as much as I hoped they would find careers with more stability, less insecurity, more genuine people, and some sense of logic, I must admit that I was pleased they were both successful.

One of the most surreal experiences I've ever had was driving down Sunset Boulevard into Hollywood one day in 2006 and seeing, first, a billboard with Tori's photo announcing her new TV series, and then, a block later, another with Randy's face overlooking Sunset, as his new series was announced. I was used to seeing famous people, but these were *my kids*! I was impressed. I bought a digital camera at the first drugstore I passed, and took pictures of both billboards. I can't look at these photos without smiling at the ingenuity and drive of my children.

But for the sake of full disclosure, I sure wouldn't mind if Tori took her career in a different direction. She and Randy both had large trust funds, and they had the means to do whatever they wanted (or not work at all). She was a great artist, and loved to paint. I knew that wasn't a secure career either, but I wanted to protect her from the rejection of a career in entertainment.

It's fine if she wants her own reality show or wants to write books about her childhood. I just wish she'd leave me out of it. I'd be glad to testify in any court of law that Tori has had a fascinating life. She has great stories to tell. She knows wonderful people. She has plenty to talk about without saying things like, "I wish I were closer to my mother" or "Did you see what my mother wrote on her Web site?"

Let me walk you through what happens every time Tori talks about me. It doesn't matter if what she says is true, if she's joking, if she's testing, or if she's just being provocative for ratings. But, of course, each of us has her own perception of reality. When Tori says the word *mother*, the focus of my life changes temporarily; and I like the normal focus better than the distractions.

I can give you a graphic example from March 2008, when Tori's book was published.

During that time I had a series of surgeries on my arm, elbow, and shoulder, and two of them coincided with Tori's TV interviews to promote her book.

During the first surgery, everywhere I turned, people were talking about Tori's media appearances. I'd never thought to check the TV schedule before planning the surgery, but I should have.

I went to a different hospital for the second surgery, on my right arm. I checked in early in the morning and was in a series of holding and prep areas prior to going to the operating room.

I knew it wasn't going to be a routine day when the bag that read PATIENT POSSESSIONS HERE started swinging for no apparent reason. Memories of an earlier hospitalization came flooding back: My phone kept ringing, and it made the locker holding my purse vibrate. It couldn't be happening again.

"Are you all right, Mrs. Spelling?" the nurse writing down my prescription medications asked. "Are you nervous? You don't need to shake. We can get you an extra blanket."

"Oh, thank you," I said. "I think my phone is vibrating, and that's making the bag swing." Sure enough, the shaking bag hanging from my hospital bed was being accompanied by a humming sound.

The nurse asked if I wanted to check for messages. I said I didn't. Anyone trying to call me at 6:15 A.M. was either a stranger or an enemy. I knew that if anything was important, the security man at my house would get word to me.

I watched the bag shake and vibrate. Then the humming was replaced by strains of "My Way," Beethoven's Ninth, "Funny Face," and "It's a Lovely Day." I realized that some of those calls were coming from friends who had been assigned their own ringtones.

The mystery of my sudden popularity was solved.

"Mrs. Spelling, look!" the nurse said. "Isn't that your daughter on TV?"

I looked up at the wall monitor, and there was Tori on a morning show. *Oh no. It can't be happening again.*

"Mrs. Spelling, she says your relationship is complicated. What does that mean?"

"I'm not sure," I said, "but I don't think she is being complimentary. Just a guess."

It was one of the longest days of my life, as Tori's publisher had booked her on one show after another, and I was having surgery. It was like the movie *Groundhog Day*, where Bill Murray experiences the same day over and over.

When I was moved into the pre-op room, I was greeted by the happy news that my new room had a television.

"Oh, you can turn it off," I said.

"Wait. Isn't that your daughter? What a pretty dress. Listen. She's talking about you."

I wanted to know when the anesthesiologist would be arriving.

"Oh, he's here somewhere," the nurse said, not taking her eyes off the TV for a second. "Why are you complicated? You seem nice to me."

"Thanks," I muttered. "Can I have drugs now?"

She laughed. "Oh, your daughter is funny when she talks about you. Did you really dress her as Marie Antoinette one Halloween? I read that somewhere."

"Yes, and she looked beautiful. She loved the costume, the wig, and jewelry, and we had so much fun doing her makeup."

"Huh," the nurse responded. "She says you forced her to be something she wasn't."

I had to agree that yes, she wasn't Marie Antoinette. Thank heaven for small favors. I'd hate to have been Marie's mother. Just thinking about it made my neck hurt. I tried to explain again.

"She loved that costume. She kept the pictures in her bedroom for years and showed them to everyone. We proudly displayed the portrait of Tori as Marie and Randy as her young Louis XVI, complete with powdered wig, in our home, and Tori would proudly show it to her friends. Where are my drugs?"

"Hi, Candy," my surgeon said when he entered my cubicle. "Guess what? I just saw Tori on TV, and she's talking about you."

On cue, my possession bag started doing its dance to "I Am Woman."

"Hi, Doctor," I said, ignoring the ringing phone. "When is my surgery?"

He told me there was no need to hurry. "Oh, Tori is on a different show now. No rush. We can move you to a later time, so you can watch the whole show."

"No," I said, way too loud for a hospital, hoping no tabloid spies were around to report that I'd screamed my head off. "I want to get this over with." He thought I meant the surgery.

By the time the anesthesiologist arrived, a little group of people had assembled to watch Tori with me.

"Oh, this is so exciting, Mrs. Spelling. It must be so great to see your child on television."

"It can be."

The hospital staff was discussing Tori's story about our giving her a BMW instead of a VW. A man sticking me with an IV needle, while watching the wall-mounted TV, said, "Oh, she must have that backward. You got her a Volkswagen when she wanted a BMW, right?"

"No," I said. "My daughter is actually complaining that her father and I bought her a new BMW—you know, one of those really safe and ultimately sporty and luxurious cars—instead of a tiny little car."

There was silence. I wouldn't have known how to respond, either.

"I have a BMW," the anesthesiologist finally said. "It's red. I love it."

"When is my surgery?" I asked meekly.

"As soon as the show is over," he told me cheerfully.

Darn.

I'd like to be able to report that the hospital scenario of that day was an aberration—but it wasn't.

When the surgery was over, Tori was on the news.

"I just wanted to be a normal kid, but my parents lived in this big house and took us to all these fancy places," were the first words I heard on the way out of the recovery room. I figured she was complaining, but I wasn't sure.

When I got the good news that I could go home, a place

where I had my own remote control and could watch whatever I wanted, I figured that my second surreal hospital day of listening to people interpret my daughter was over. I was wrong.

When we got to the parking lot, a woman wanted to know if I was "that Mrs. Spelling."

"Hi. I'm Candy Spelling," I said.

"Why did you give your daughter only eight hundred thousand dollars when her father died? What kind of mother are you?"

I knew I couldn't get any more drugs, but I did see my car approaching. I leaped from my wheelchair and into the car. Had she really said, *"only* eight hundred thousand"?

I thought about going back and explaining to this complete stranger that she was so wrong, how wills worked, that eight hundred thousand was an inaccurate number, that Tori was fine and had plenty of money, that she and her family were provided for. Both the kids had large trust funds and had never worried about, or probably even thought about, money. I wanted to ask her if she had seen Tori's supposed "garage sale," and had stopped to think about the number of possessions Tori had amassed. She took just some of her possessions out of storage and still had so much furniture, clothing, gifts, appliances, jewelry, shoes, and, of course, dog clothing that she made thousands and thousands of dollars. Tori always had money, and was making millions of dollars.

But I didn't want to get into a discussion with a stranger

in a hospital parking lot about how much money my daughter had inherited.

At home my voice mail was full with messages telling me not only what shows Tori had been on, but also much of what she'd said.

My nicest friend whispered into my voice mail, "I don't think a complicated relationship is that bad. Hope your surgery went well."

My closest friend said, "Just let me know if you want to leave the country until the book tour is over. I'll go with you, but I don't want to go to Asia. It's too long a flight."

Others left messages including, "Oh, you poor thing. You are such a good mother"; "Tori must be in a really bad mood today"; and "Tori found out she could make a living talking about you. This is like Joan Rivers and her Edgar, and those poor ex-wives of Johnny Carson. Ouch."

I hadn't been married to one of Hollywood's greatest showmen for decades without figuring out that the publication of Tori's book had been timed to promote the new season of her TV show, and vice versa. So, although there was a brief lull, I knew there was more to come.

Tori's reality show was moving from its setting at an inn to her home in Hollywood. So, without having to worry about feeding guests and cleaning rooms, she would now have fewer concerns and more time to talk about me.

Darn.

Fade to the start of the new TV season.

Now when my home phone lines light up all at once and my cell phone begins belting out show tunes, I know Tori's on television again.

Sure enough, the night her show made its debut, my phones went crazy. Every time zone reported in, hour after hour, so by the time a show had run at ten P.M. in L.A., I had had a full report.

"Oh, Tori wishes you guys were closer" seemed to be the consensus. That was from people who knew my phone numbers.

What I never imagined was the uniquely twenty-first-century phenomenon of everyone having access to everyone else, otherwise known as e-mail.

The man who operates my Web site faxed me a cryptic message.

Mrs. Spelling,

   Your email is going crazy. Is everything all right? It will take a few days to forward it all. I'm sorry.

   TMS

I figured my spam filter—whatever that was—wasn't working.

No. It was people who'd watched or heard Tori talking about us and had decided to contact me directly.

Nothing prepared me for what came next.

Thousands of e-mails later, from all parts of the country,

from people of all ages, grandmothers and grandchildren, psychologists and steelworkers, I heard from all of America.

Some were downright nasty.

> You are heartless. How much money do you need? Your daughter needs money. Give it to her,

wrote a stranger who said she was from Dixie.

I wondered if the woman from Dixie would care that I'd set up multimillion-dollar trust funds and education funds for my grandchildren, just like Aaron and I did for Tori and Randy. Probably not. The next week this one came:

> I think you are a b————, and I think a magazine will name you worst mother of the year. If you gave your children money, you should continue to give them as much when they grow up.

That woman had marked her e-mail "urgent."

I wondered if the e-mailer ever thought about how all the inns, houses, luxury SUVs, vacations, clothes, furniture, toys, parties, caterers, gifts, and everything else highlighted on Tori's show had been paid for. Memo to writer: Tori has lots of money, and she spends it on whatever she wants.

Some e-mails were sweet:

> I have been watching your daughter's show, but I truly believe you are a wonderful Mother and Person. I think she complains too

much just for the television cameras. You have wonderful advice
for others, like good mothers do,

wrote a woman who said she was Tori's age.

I love all your husband's TV series. Like some of the characters
on his shows, I think you are misunderstood. If you write a biography, I will definitely read it. I want to know more,

was the sweet message that arrived from a woman who said
she hoped to be a grandmother soon.

Many messages took the middle of the road, like the following one, from a man who admitted to being a constant TV
watcher.

I didn't know too much about your family until I watched some
episodes of Tori's TV show. That sent me to your Web site, and I
love it! I think that, despite how much Tori complains, she obviously loves and needs you, and she also loves and needs drama
and to be the center of attention. I think anyone who the public
knows for the love and kindness you have is someone I want to
know. Will you get your own show and write a book?

Almost everyone had an opinion. I was a good mother.
I was a terrible mother. Tori was a good daughter. Tori
was a terrible mother and daughter. Her husband, Dean,
should take off his glasses. Dean should shave. My grandson,

Liam, is adorable, but he should be eating less and sleeping more.

Week after week, talk show appearance after talk show appearance, Tuesday night meant my Web site crashing and the webmaster losing sleep.

Many people demanded to know "everything" about our family's finances. Others had memories of my husband's shows. Some said they couldn't imagine their own children talking about them on television week after week. A few people sent photos of their families and pets for me to see.

I answered most of them. At the time, I didn't reply to the stories Tori told. I'm the mature mother, I had to keep reminding myself. I replied to some of the stories people told me about themselves and their families. I was asked for a lot of advice about fields I know nothing about, and was sorry I couldn't help. My ego expanded one moment when some praised my charity work; and the next e-mail made me think, Who the heck does this stranger think she is, saying these nasty things about me when she doesn't even know me?

I'm not sure what Tori means when she says our relationship is complicated. I wish she would call me, rather than say on television, "I should call my mom." I wish she'd tell me that she was unhappy about something that happened when she was in the sixth grade that I thought was a highlight of her life.

Tori does usually end her dissertations about our life with "We love each other."

We do. And we always will.

Chapter 5

The Sounds of Silence: Golden or Dangerous?

One of the first maxims I remember learning is "Silence is golden." I don't recall if I learned it before I found out "Children should be seen and not heard," but, whatever the order, I got the message.

It was all right with me. I was painfully shy, and I was relieved that silence was a virtue. So I could be golden and well behaved by being shy, instead of being labeled as having some social deficiency.

It hurt a lot when people said I was "cold" or "snobbish" or "haughty" or just "antisocial." I wanted to tell them I was just painfully shy, but I was much too timid and insecure to break into their conversations, even when they were about me.

Over the years, I realized that my shyness enabled me to hone my listening skills. I knew I had to be a good listener because I needed to make sure I'd be right if and when I spoke. So I paid attention to every conversation to make sure I wouldn't make a mistake when I gathered the courage to be part of the discussion.

I knew I had allies when I first heard the words of a 1964 hit song by the Four Seasons. I decided it would become my secret anthem.

> *Silence is golden, but my eyes still see*
> *Silence is golden, golden*
> *But my eyes still see.*
> *Talking is cheap, people follow like sheep . . .*

So, rather than being a cheap sheep follower, I listened and tried to learn.

I have to admit I was conflicted when Simon and Garfunkel's 1966 warning to my generation hit the charts. So, with apologies to Paul Simon, who wrote:

The Sounds of Silence: Golden or Dangerous?

"Fools," said I, "you do not know
Silence like a cancer grows."

. . . silence can be good for some of us.

One unexpected and very positive reaction to my years of silent shyness is that I developed a sense of security over time that permits me to go out by myself and do things alone.

Most of my friends, who are not the least bit shy, would be afraid to be seen alone in a restaurant or movie. Not me. I don't mind the occasional solitude. More than that, I often learn things I'd never know if I were part of a group.

I'd like to think I'm attentive, curious, and patient, not just that I have excellent hearing. Hopefully, it's a combination of all those assets.

When I go to restaurants by myself, it's by choice. I have a lot of friends, so it's not lack of opportunity. I just really enjoy learning from watching and listening to other people in restaurants.

I know I caught some network executives off guard in a recent meeting when one of them started explaining "webisodes" to me.

"Wait," I said. "I know all about webisodes."

I first heard about webisodes when, in between bites of sushi, I overheard two TV honchos discussing this new development over dinner at Hamasaku in Los Angeles. I thought it was such a funny word, and knew that Aaron would have jumped right into their conversation.

So, just to show how far I'd come in my being-alone-is-okay period, I asked these two strangers questions about webisodes.

"You look very familiar," the executive in the Ralph Lauren jacket said.

"Aren't you someone?" his dinner companion asked.

He, obviously, had never learned the virtue of silence.

"My husband used to work in television. My name is Candy Spelling."

"You're kidding. Aaron Spelling's wife! I'm so honored," the Polo devotee said. His friend smiled, realizing, I guess, that I was "someone."

And then they explained webisodes to me.

So, a few weeks later, I was prepared for the network guys in my meeting. In a very condescending tone, one of the online wizards began by asking me if I had a computer.

"Yes, several," I said.

"Okay. Well, sometimes, if you watch little episodes of things, you might be watching webisodes."

I smiled and said I knew about webisodes. I told them everything I'd learned while enjoying my sushi that night at the restaurant.

They were silent. My overhearing had made me heard.

Throughout my childhood, I was never really encouraged to know or say too much. My parents were protective of me, and as long as my cooking, sewing, and social skills were progressing, all was fine.

The Sounds of Silence: Golden or Dangerous?

I didn't have much incentive to study the classics, but I do remember reading Shakespeare in high school. One line resonated from *Much Ado About Nothing*:

> *Silence is the perfectest herald of joy.*
> *I were but little happy,*
> *if I could say how much.*

It sounded like Shakespeare was encouraging my journey toward perfection through silence. I liked that.

My husband was a wonderful man, but he really did consider me what later was dubbed a "trophy wife." He didn't want me to have friends, talk to strangers (unless they were *his* strangers), or interact more than superficially with the people with whom he worked. I was *his*. My knowledge was his (ours?). I was supposed to look good, smile, entertain when asked, and be his Hollywood wife.

At home, with the kids, it was different. We made decisions together, I was in charge of almost everything he took for granted, and we worked together on all aspects of his business. But my public "image" was as quiet, happy Candy, Aaron's perfect wife.

I tried hard. I think I succeeded.

He wouldn't have liked me asking strangers about webisodes or telling network executives all that I knew about their area of expertise. But now I do what I think is right, more than what is just expected or anticipated of, um, "a woman in my position"—whatever that means. Thus, this book.

I can't count how many times I overheard him being asked if *Dynasty* was about our family, or if I was the model for Linda Evans's sweet and innocent Krystle Carrington or Joan Collins's ruthless, conniving, nasty Alexis. Aaron would credit me for helping design the shows, but he said neither character was "my Candy."

My answer is that I'm neither and both characters. Linda and I looked alike, and I was able to contribute to her look. Many of Nolan Miller's clothes were based on my tastes and ideas about the look of those glamorous and trendsetting characters. But I consider myself a sharp businesswoman like Alexis, albeit much nicer and without the heavy-handed and ruthless need to rule the world.

In personality, I was closer to quiet Krystle than attention-seeking Alexis. Whenever the script called for Krystle to speak out, I wondered if Aaron was afraid his Candy would someday speak out, too. He didn't have to worry. I kept quiet in public, and certainly never exhibited any of the drama and angst of the *Dynasty* characters. In private, he and I were truly partners—again, minus the angst and drama of the TV heroines and vixens.

Aaron loved telling people the story about the diamond that Blake gave Krystle.

"Candy was on the set when someone brought out the diamond ring John Forsythe was giving to Linda Evans on that week's episode. Candy jumped up from her chair and said, 'He would never buy her such a tiny ring. Get a bigger one.' We had to stop production while Candy and the wardrobe people went out and found the perfect ring for the show.

"She was right. You wouldn't believe how many viewers wrote letters about the ring and how it was the ultimate piece of jewelry for Krystle."

My mother had taught me well about jewelry.

One of the most difficult times to maintain my silence was when Tori asked Nolan to design her a "dress with breasts." My little girl was just seven. Aaron thought it was cute. Nolan was happy to oblige.

My mother and I never talked about "breasts," and now my daughter wanted Hollywood's top designer to make a pair for her attached to a grown-up dress. Yikes! I'll bet Dr. Spock wouldn't have had an answer for that one, and Dr. Ruth and Sue Johanson weren't famous enough for me to know about them yet. Dear Abby lived nearby, but I knew Aaron wouldn't like it if I asked her what to do.

I experienced that helpless feeling, as though I was a little seven-year-old in school, withdrawn and not knowing what to say. This time I wanted to be the right 1970s mother, not 1950s classmate, but it felt the same. What was the right answer? What would a "good" mother do? Did Aaron have any "good mothers" on his television shows? Anyone like Donna Reed, or Mrs. Walton, or even Jane Jetson? I couldn't think of any.

Tori got her dress. I still haven't recovered from the shock of seeing her in that dress and holding a cigarette. I flashed on the old Kodak commercial and the song "Turn Around":

> *Where are you going,*
> *My little one, little one . . .*

Aaron liked to have me visit the sets, and when I did, my shyness zoomed into high gear. Right after we were married, he was working on a show called *New People*, which was shooting at Zuma Beach. I went to the location, and we stayed at a little motel near the water.

Our first night there he told me, "Candy, I want to show you off."

"I can't. I have to clean."

I'm still not sure if the motel bathroom was so terrible that I needed to use Lysol all over it, or if I just cleaned to avoid meeting new people. Anyway, I chose being a good wife over a silly social occasion, and our room was cleaner than anyone else's.

It rained the next day, yet Aaron insisted I stop cleaning and come to the set. He sent a man over with a yellow rain slicker. I was certain my new husband hadn't seen it. He wouldn't have liked the way I looked in it.

But my appearance wasn't his main concern.

"Did you return it to wardrobe?" he later asked.

"Of course. Why would I want an ugly men's slicker?" I forgot my "silence is golden" lessons with that answer. He didn't say anything, but I took care not to reply like that often during our long marriage.

I stayed silent when Aaron told me that Stefanie Powers had declared that she did not want Nolan Miller on the set of *Hart to Hart*, and that she didn't like his designs. Ouch. "He's not allowed," she said. Remarkably, my husband—her boss—agreed to her demand, although not for long. I figured he knew his actors better than I did, and his track record told me he was making the right move.

I also listened in amazement and disbelief when Aaron told me that Kate Jackson had banned him from the set of *Charlie's Angels*, although I didn't stay silent. "Wait, Aaron, you're the boss. It's your show." He nodded and assured me "it would work out." It wasn't the first or the last of the diva stories from the set of *Charlie's Angels*, and he ignored Jackson's soon-forgotten command for him to stay away.

I often wanted to counsel others to be a bit more discreet, too. In that period, the tabloids were evolving from reporting stories of three-headed, sixteen-toed monsters from another planet to printing juicy details about what the stars said and did (or didn't say and do). I wished some of his stars were less prominent in the tabloids, but Aaron assured me it only helped the shows they were on. He told me his public relations people were not allowed to speak to the tabloids, except once a year, when they published their television preview issues. Everyone cooperated then, to promote the fall series. I didn't comment about the obvious double standard in this, even though I disliked the concept.

On Friday nights, when the shows were taping, I often played poker with the crew during the long breaks some of them had. Boy, was that a great place for gossip! I was so quiet, and I think some of the guys sometimes forgot who I was. That's when I was happiest, being Candy, not "the Mrs."

"You have to stop winning at poker," Aaron warned me. "The crew gets really mad when you win."

✄

People always thought Aaron and I lived the life of *Dynasty*. More than once, while entertaining overnight guests, we would be waiting for the houseguest to come join us in the kitchen for breakfast, only to find the guest waiting in his or her room for "breakfast in bed." "That's how it works on Aaron's shows," one British studio executive and one-time houseguest told me. "I assumed that's how you would treat your houseguests." He soon moved to a hotel.

The designer Nolan Miller had a secret distinction in Aaron's and my life. He was the houseguest who wouldn't leave. He stayed seven and a half years. At first it was fun to hear his great stories, and at the beginning, he would bring beautiful flowers home for us. Then we began talking about his leaving. He even owned an apartment building where he said he was going to live, but had never completed what he said was the necessary construction. In time, it was clear to all of us that he should move out. According to my count, he lived with us for 2,739 days, and we fed him more than 6,000 meals. He left with a classic 1965 Rolls-Royce Silver Cloud, which Aaron and I bought for him as a present because he'd told us it was his "life's dream."

❈

Aaron's brother, Danny, once asked why we hadn't introduced him to the cook, so he could give him a list of what he wanted for every meal. "We don't have a cook now, Danny," I explained. "I cook for Aaron and the kids."

He seemed disappointed. But when I cooked for him, too, he seemed to mind less.

❈

While Aaron and I were dating, I visited the set of *The Mod Squad*. I had taken the afternoon off from my sales job at Joseph Magnin, and I wanted to see Aaron. I also had a brand-new car I could barely afford—a four-day-old silver 1966 Corvette—and I couldn't wait to drive it on to the studio lot.

I know my choice of car was odd for someone who was trying to blend in. But I had a good job, life was good, and I felt I had achieved some success. In L.A., a car was the ultimate status symbol, and I loved mine. The Corvette was the first new car I'd ever had, and I was acting like a responsible adult with it, making the payments on the dream vehicle.

I parked the car carefully and went to find Aaron. Just as I was greeting him, I heard a crash. Out of nowhere, a small studio crane had dropped its load and punched a hole into the fiberglass hood of my brand-new sports car! Everyone gathered around to see what had happened.

"Everybody, meet Candy Marer," Aaron said, beaming. "This is the girl I'm going to marry." I don't know if I was more horrified at my wrecked car or at being introduced to a group of strangers.

At least no one expected me to speak.

"She's such a good sport," one of the camera operators said. "She's not even yelling. My girlfriend would be scream-ing."

Fortunately, the production company had insurance, and my Corvette was repaired.

The Corvette incident was symbolic of Aaron's and my relationship. We never yelled or screamed at each other, and rarely had arguments. Aaron liked to show me off.

As Aaron became more successful, money to fix—or buy—cars became inconsequential. Our discussions about money were basically about how to give our kids everything they should have without giving them a sense of entitle-ment. We'd witnessed Hollywood and other affluent families whose children spent money capriciously and recklessly, and we wanted Tori and Randy to grow up to be responsible and knowledgable about finances.

Tori was a Brownie, Girl Scout, aspiring ice skater, horseback rider, rabbit breeder, and grunion-running hater. Randy played T-ball, Little League, collected baseball cards, took tennis lessons, and was a video game expert. If it sounds "normal," it's because their school lives and extracurricular activities were like those of every other child. I was a room mother at their school. I sat through dance lessons, consoled Randy when his tennis coach upset him. We were strict disciplinarians about bedtimes, homework, phone restrictions, and curfews. They weren't Hollywood kids. They were American kids. We were together almost all the time, either at home, on the beach, or on family outings.

My respect for silence served me well during my marriage. Early on I decided that there was no sense in arguing with my husband. He was a wordsmith, and I had spent years being afraid to speak. I wouldn't have had a chance with him. I couldn't win.

It was just as well. We loved each other, and we were one of the few Hollywood couples who avoided tabloid coverage over family arguments.

Thanks to the Four Seasons and William Shakespeare for the encouragement, and to Thomas Carlyle, whose words pulled me through my self-consciousness when he wrote, "Silence is more eloquent than words."

Chapter 6

❊

Celebrity Houses and Glue Guns Require a Gift-Wrapping Room

As a girl I was as fascinated as anyone by "celebrities," but even though I grew up in Los Angeles, my family was not in the entertainment industry, so I had little exposure to the "stars." I studied—sometimes memorized—my movie magazines, and dreamed of Ricky Nelson or Elvis Presley someday singing to me, thanks in part to the beauty tips Elizabeth Taylor, Lana Turner, Audrey Hepburn, and Ingrid Bergman generously shared with me through these fan magazines.

And then I became a celebrity wife. In Hollywood terms, I'm a celebrity by marriage and a celebrity by motherhood. And in the "industry," that makes me a celebrity.

Celebrities get way too much attention and credit, but they certainly sell movies, music, products, and all forms of entertainment. Thanks to more TV stations, reality shows, and the Internet, there are more celebrities than ever before, although not all of them will be as enduring as those I grew up loving.

There's a big celebrity culture that you'd have to be here in L.A. to appreciate or truly understand. There are celebrity shoppers and stylists, shoemakers to the stars, top entertainment valet parkers, lots of star hairdressers and makeup artists, supermarkets and restaurants where celebrities supposedly gather, leading celebrity dog groomers (I think the dogs belong to the celebrities, but maybe it's "celebrity dogs"), and many more.

Being a celebrity, knowing celebrities, working with celebrities, writing about celebrities, feeding celebrities, repairing celebrity cars, and photographing celebrities—these are just some of the elements of our local economy. There is no end to the public's fascination with all things (and people) celebrity.

Do you remember Sally Field's often-misquoted "You like me . . . you really like me!" cry at the 1985 Academy Awards? (She actually said, "I can't deny the fact that you like me, right now, you like me.")

I understand what she meant. Celebrities (and celebrities by marriage and motherhood) are never quite sure if people like them for themselves, or because they just want to be part of the celebrity world.

And that's where my house comes in. I live in a "celebrity house."

I knew we were asking for it, building the largest home in Los Angeles. We didn't set out to build the largest home. In fact, because I couldn't read blueprints, I was often surprised by what was eventually built. I had no concept of how the size on the blueprints translated to actual size. My gift-wrapping room should have been larger, and two of the powder rooms could use more space. My office could have been a lot smaller. I kept adjusting my guesses as I saw the room sizes. It was far from a scientific way to operate, but we were so happy with it. We just wanted a great house that had everything we'd dreamed about. We knew how fortunate we were that years of success in television were allowing us to live out our dreams.

I'd like to explain some misconceptions about our house.

First, yes, it is called Spelling Manor, or just The Manor. It was built on the site of the old Bing Crosby house, and "Crosby Teardown" just didn't resonate.

Second, it does not have 123 rooms. I don't know where that number came from, but it's not that many; and I refuse to count the rooms. It's better to truly be able to say, "I don't know." I can say there are many rooms in my 56,500 square feet of living space and 17,000-square-foot attic on our five-acre property.

Third, yes, there is a bowling alley in our basement. My husband loved to bowl, and he found it quite relaxing. But when we were building the house, there weren't very many local places to bowl, and as more and more people found out Aaron loved to relax by bowling, anytime he entered a bowling alley, he would be barraged with head shots, videotapes, résumés, and lists of credits by people aspiring to acting careers. One night, an aspiring actor actually jumped into Aaron's lane while he was getting ready to bowl and started reciting lines from a *Starsky & Hutch* episode. Aaron never recovered. That night, he proclaimed that our new house would have to have its own bowling alley.

He really liked the bowling alley, and our family and friends often hung out there. We had a big sectional couch on a raised platform behind the scoring table, and two lanes for the rooting section; and a lot of Aaron's favorite awards, photos, and memorabilia were on display there. We also had a closet of bowling shoes in every size for men, women, and children. Well, we thought we had every size—until Tom Selleck came to bowl one night. We didn't have shoes large enough for him that first time, but we did for his next visit. I think Tom won with and without bowling shoes. I was watching, but not keeping score. Anyway, Aaron didn't miss a chance to challenge a guest. We even had special red-and-green bowling balls we would move down from the attic and into the bowling alley every December.

Next, I have three gift-wrapping rooms. When people visit for the first time, they almost always ask to see the gift-wrapping room. I show them my favorite space, a fifteen-by-fourteen-foot room adjacent to my office and near the kitchen door. Our companies often employed a thousand or more people, and Aaron worked with hundreds more at the networks, studios, talent, and PR agencies and elsewhere. Holidays aside, when we had thousands of gifts to give, we often had a few gifts a day to wrap. I love selecting gifts and wrapping, and I even opened a gift and wrapping store in Beverly Hills with a partner, Lehr and Spelling. I had to give it up, though, because there was too much happening with building the house; my running a business at the same time was too much for Aaron. So it was logical and practical to have a room dedicated to wrapping and distributing gifts. I have dozens of rolls of paper, hundreds of ribbons and bows, thousands of different decorations to individualize each package, glue guns, scissors, tape, and bubble wrap, and I never stop buying cards and fun souvenirs to put on the gifts.

Just for the record, my two other gift-wrapping rooms are more industrial-size, for big packages, and equipped to rival any professional mailing center.

And, yes, Tori and I did once change my grandson Liam's diaper on the table in my gift-wrapping room. We were

walking to the kitchen when she realized he needed his diaper changed. The flat table in the gift-wrapping room was
the perfect surface.

So, I'll admit that the bowling alley and gift-wrapping
room add to my house being classified as a "celebrity house."

But there's more.

On an average summer day, tour buses stop in front of
my house at least every ten minutes. I hear the microphones
and megaphones:

*"It's the largest house in Los Angeles, with one hundred
and twenty-three rooms."*

Wrong (except for the largest house part).

"It's the house where Tori Spelling grew up."

Wrong. (She lived in that house for a very short time. She
actually spent most of her life in our previous house, also on
the same street but a few blocks away.)

"There's a full-size bowling alley in the living room."

Wrong.

"The house is for sale for one billion dollars."

I wish.

"Dynasty was shot in this house."

Wrong.

The house has quite a reputation to maintain.

⌘

Celebrities, whether people or houses, have to be on guard
all the time. One bad photo can wreck an image, or maybe

even a career. Celebrities have to put on makeup when they go out, to avoid a bad photo getting taken. We rush any repair trucks in through a service gate before the tourists can spot that we, too, have plumbing problems. It's all about the image, darlings.

Before Tori and Randy established their own careers, they, too, were celebrities by birth. It was sometimes difficult to keep them grounded, and harder to make them understand that many of their life experiences were unique to them.

I always wondered what our kids thought when strangers walked up to Aaron and said, "I love you" or "I love your work."

I can't count how many people approached them as children to tell them their favorite episodes of *Dynasty* or *The Love Boat*, and recited dialogue line by line. Our kids rarely watched those shows, as they were on too late, but I was always proud at how polite they were at these times.

Tori always felt important when someone asked her to sign a napkin when we were out to dinner. She liked being the center of attention.

Randy, too, would accommodate strangers who asked to have their picture taken with him, although I'm not sure he knew why.

I still haven't recovered from the first time someone in a public ladies' room asked me to autograph a paper towel and address it to "Tifany with one *f*." I dried my hands first and then tried to explain to Tori, who was with me, why I was signing a paper towel. I don't remember how I explained it.

I spent a lot of time explaining to the kids that some people would be nice to them because they thought they might get something from them. It wasn't a message I wanted to give my children, but often it was true. I would point out the flaws I saw in some of their so-called friends, but they got angry with me and questioned my motives. Some of the teens they were friends with ordered my staff around. One houseman refused to serve some of Tori's friends because, as he told me, "there was a distinct lack of manners and a collective sense of entitlement." One night, two of Randy's friends ended up in Tori's bedroom. Tori was no longer living at home, but that didn't make it any easier when I found them in her bed, the girl looking at me coyly as she puffed on a cigarette. My own kids weren't like that.

I didn't like it when the children were mad at me, so I'd usually give in when those same "friends" of theirs persuaded them to hold parties at our house. I either allowed the parties (and cooked and prepared for them) or risked alienating my children. Suffice it to say we had a lot of teen parties at The Manor. Tori was in full teenage mode when we moved into the house, and Randy became quite a host, too.

Expectations are always high, and that's especially true with my house. People who visit don't know if they'll see Scarlett O'Hara's Tara before the Civil War, the Carrington

House during a black-tie party, or the Beverly Hillbillies' mansion.

My insecurities rage when I invite people to The Manor. I'm afraid they'll find something they won't like, afraid they only want to see the house, not be with me. Maybe it's too many years as a celebrity by accident?

At the end of 2007, I took a deep breath and decided to have a holiday party. I spent weeks working with the so-called "celebrity" party planners, caterers, assistants, artists, chefs, tree decorators, and others to make sure everything was perfect. I hadn't entertained in a long time, first because my husband had been ill for years, and, after he passed away, because I didn't feel like socializing. But I decided it was time. . . .

I spent weeks agonizing over every detail of the décor, food, invitation, table settings, songs the piano players would perform, making sure everything was perfect for the 140 guests I was inviting. All 180 boxes of my Christmas decorations were used, from holly to adorn the lamppost at the bottom of the driveway, to hundreds of toy soldiers standing at attention outside the front door, to the antique ornaments on the trees and stuffed animals carefully placed on the staircase, to even miniature holiday decorations in my doll museum.

And then there was the candy. How can Candy not have the right candy? I collect candy jars, candy dishes, candy dispensers, and antique candy machines, so my guests can have their choice of candy. As long as I've been entertaining at home, I've felt I would be judged on my candy (and lots of other things, as you now know). The afternoon of my party, I realized I hadn't taken care of the candy. I bought thousands of calories of goodies—hundreds of little candy bars with all our favorite childhood brands, Hershey's Kisses, M&Ms (plain and peanut), Snickers, Hershey bars, bags of Sour Patch Kids, chocolate-covered raisins, almonds covered in chocolate, boxes of See's mixed nuts, jelly beans, white Jordan almonds, Mary Janes, malted balls, Dots, plus peanuts and pretzels—but I hadn't relegated each to its proper place. I filled two dozen candy dishes and jars with a variety of candy, and put them everywhere, where people would be doing everything from singing karaoke to sampling caviar. I ran around so much and so fast to get it all done that I rewarded myself with two handfuls of M&Ms, a Crunch bar, some Sour Patch Kids, and nut and candy combinations. I figured I had worked off just that many calories.

About an hour before my first guests arrived, one of the party planners was giving the servers a tour of the various rooms where food was being set up. He was also pointing out the downstairs bathrooms, in case guests asked for them.

I walked by as he was pointing to a powder room just outside the family room. "There's a smaller bathroom," he said. I watched as they all examined the bathroom. "Yes," I heard one server say to the woman next to him. "That one is smaller, almost like a regular bathroom."

Being Candy, I felt terrible about having a "smaller" bathroom. Darn. If only I had learned how to read blueprints. I was wounded. With all the great food, beautiful decorations, and wonderful music and games, this server would remember a small bathroom. And being a celebrity by accident, I feared that the tabloids would run a story about the tiny guest bathrooms in the Spelling household.

My guests were generous with superlatives about the menu, holiday decorations, ice sculptures, special lighting, entertainment, gorgeous trees, and even the snow we had arranged to fall outside the living room windows. Technicians had put a big machine and compressor on the roof, and snowblowing machines were positioned to make big snowflakes. The lighting was beautiful, too, highlighting the prop snow. I loved it because it was truly out of a Hollywood movie.

Lots of people visited the first-floor gift-wrapping room, and all sizes of bowling shoes and Christmas-colored bowling balls were used for the first time in years. Others played poker, some used the video arcade, professional singers performed karaoke, and everyone had a good time.

The tabloids never reported a word about any of the bathrooms. And not one guest said a word about one of the bathrooms being smaller than the others.

They liked my house; they really liked it. My house's celebrity reputation remains intact.

Chapter 7

❀

Stop, Look, and Listen to My Dog

I think Spot, the dog who belonged to Dick and Jane and their family, was the smartest member of the household.

This idea initially came to me in the first grade, and my belief was reinforced chapter by chapter, book by book.

In the story "Dick and Spot," Dick and Spot are walking home from the grocery store.

"Look, Spot, look.

"Look and see.

"Stop, stop."

This is exactly what Dick says to his loyal canine when Dick's little cap blows off his head and into the busy street.

Then, when the light at the corner turns green, Dick commands:

"Go, Spot.

"Go, Spot, go."

Spot zooms into the street and retrieves Dick's cap. Dick says,

"Look, look.

"See Spot.

"Come, Spot, come."

But Spot is already there, cap in mouth.

I was told from a very young age that dogs were color-blind. So how was Spot supposed to figure out that he was to stop when the light was red and go when it was green? And he must have been confused further by Dick saying, "Come, Spot, come," when he was already there.

Dick lost his cap. Spot retrieved it from a street and brought it back. Who's smarter?

In "Guess Who," the family spends most of the time talking to the dog:

"Oh, Spot.

"Did you see my ball?

"Where is it, Spot?

"Go get it."

The red ball is in full view, yet Spot is the only family member able to find it. He brings it over. No one even thanks him.

Spot brought in clothes from the clothesline when it started raining without saying a word. The rest of the family was pointing at one another and giving weather reports.

Spot is the first one into the family car for a trip, thus avoiding having to carry anything heavy.

In "Who Can Help," Dick is again carrying groceries, but this time without a cap, and Spot is waiting inside the house.

Spot watches and listens as Dick says:

"Mother, Mother.

"Come here.

"I want you.

"Come and help me.

"Oh, Jane.

"Oh, Father.

"Who can come?

"Who can come and help me?"

The monologue continues. Spot is obviously thinking, "Dick, just put down one of the bags and open the door yourself."

Instead, Dick decides:

"Little Spot can help me.

"You can help me come in."

And he does.

When I got home from school, I watched other smart dogs. Lassie always saved the day, Rin Tin Tin saved the West, and Bullet saved Roy Rogers, Dale Evans, and their friends.

Back at school, I would read all about this family who spoke mostly in single syllables and asked questions, but rarely did anything. They needed Spot to find the ball or open the door or run into traffic for them.

Growing up, I was allowed only one dog. I was eight years old, and my parents gave me Sammy, my first true love (other than Rock Hudson), a handsome beige-and-black pug. We were inseparable. I'd walk him down our street every day, and I could tell he really enjoyed getting to know the lawns on our block. His tail didn't curve, and he wasn't wrinkled like most pugs, but it didn't matter; he was my Sammy. I thought he'd grow into his curves and wrinkles, like people did.

Unfortunately, Sammy and I didn't get to grow up together. When we went to Palm Springs for Easter, my mother's hairdresser, Bessie, offered to watch Sammy. When we got home,

Sammy wasn't there. My parents told me he had heart problems, which they said explained why his tail didn't curl. The problems got worse, they said, and he had died of a heart attack while we were away. The truth was he had been injured in an accident and died, but I didn't find that out until years later.

I was heartbroken. I was hysterical. There was no consoling me. Sammy was my best friend, and now he was mysteriously gone. My mother was so distraught by my sadness and grief that she said I would never be allowed to have another dog. "You can have all the dogs you want when you grow up," she promised. When I was eight, I couldn't imagine being grown up enough to have my own dogs. I only wanted Sammy. Reading about Spot made me sad. I wanted someone like Spot or Lassie to watch over my family, and we had no one.

My mother kept her promise not to let me have another dog, but as soon as I was on my own, I started adopting dogs.

When the kids were little we had as many as six at a time. That was the first time we bought an "extra-large California king-size bed." We had all sizes, every mix: purebreds, barkers, lickers, jumpers, each one more loving and special than the next.

Most of them had stories. Pepper came home with Tori when she was a guest star on *Fantasy Island*. She had told me she was working with an adorable terrier mix, but never mentioned a word about bringing it home. She and Aaron walked in one night and introduced me to "our" new dog. "Oh, no," I said. "We have a whole houseful already."

"But, Mom," Tori said, "he's a present from Ricardo Montalban, so I had to take him."

"Yes, Candy," Aaron added, "Ricardo gave Pepper to Tori. I couldn't say no."

Pepper started out as Tori's, but like all the others, he soon became a family dog. Then Randy wanted Tiffany, a bichon frise. She was exclusively Randy's for three weeks, and then joined the ranks of family dogs.

Shelley was another bichon frise, and not to belittle the others, not only did we love her dearly, but she was the best dog ever. She never stopped entertaining us, and was truly funny. Everyone loved Shelley, and she loved everyone. Shelley soon became best friends with Muffin, our apricot poodle.

We always loved dogs. One of our saddest days was at the pet cemetery when Tori insisted on a funeral for Vic, one of our dachshunds. (We also had Trola, as in Victrola. Get it?) The dachshunds' most memorable feat—other than being lovable—was ganging up on Angel, our white poodle. Angel, though, got back at them. She did tricks, and everyone who visited us would head right for Angel to say hello.

My last dog before my current dog, Madison, was Annie, a wonderful terrier mix who passed away suddenly last year from a pancreatic attack. She was only ten, and she had been with me for almost nine years, since I rescued her from a puppy mill.

Annie liked to hang out with my security guards. There was always someone ready to play with her, and she had a great view of my driveway. The security room has a wall of monitors that show different views of my house and beach house. I never saw Annie pay much attention to the monitors. Her job, at least how she defined it, was to entertain the security staff and keep an eye on the driveway.

One morning Annie started barking furiously at one of the monitors. The guard on duty tried to quiet her down, pointing out that there was no one outside. He then realized she was looking up at the monitor that had views of my beach house. Inside the house was—hmm, how should I put this?—an ex-friend of mine. I hadn't seen him for months. Summoned to the security room, I asked them why Annie was barking. "You'll see," he said, pointing to a monitor.

There was my ex-friend wandering around the beach house, moving from camera to camera, obviously not knowing he was being watched. My guard called the beach house to see if the guy would pick up the phone. He didn't. The guard then called my ex-friend's cell phone.

We watched the monitor as my ex-friend answered his cell phone and my guard told him that an alarm had gone off and he wanted to make sure everything was all right. His eyes darted around the room; it was clear he had spotted one of the cameras. He stammered, "Why are you calling me? I'm home," he lied. "I was sleeping." The guard apologized and shrugged his shoulders. I laughed. Annie seemed proud.

Annie was not only smart like Spot and Lassie, but she was a great judge of people, too.

After my husband passed away, I had to have appraisals done on our home and some of our property. My lawyer lined up the foremost experts and offered to send them to the house for me to interview.

No, I thought, there's nothing I like about this whole process. While there's nothing wrong with appraisers, this was happening because I'd lost my husband, and the last thing I wanted to do was conduct business at home around his passing.

I decided I'd interview these experts at my lawyer's office in Century City, and back-to-back appointments were scheduled. I knew they would all say the same thing, and that probably all were adequately qualified. What I really wanted to see was who was the most sincere. Hollywood is full of characters and con artists. I wanted the real deal, and I knew Annie could distinguish among the candidates who would spend a lot of time in my house seriously assessing Aaron's and my life and possessions. So I brought Annie with me to the interviews.

When the building's security guard saw Annie, he stopped me, something I hadn't counted on. I instantly remembered a joke from Bette Midler's show about her pretending her dog was a Seeing Eye dog, but I couldn't pull that off.

"She has to go into the building," I told the guard. "We're going to the lawyer's office because she is the beneficiary of a will. The reading is today, and she has to be there."

The guard was speechless. I was proud. Annie and I got into the elevator.

Sure enough, the decision about whom to hire became clear. Even without a scorecard, without a word or a look, Annie's body language told me which expert to choose. She let me know whom she would welcome into our home. We hired the appraiser on the spot.

I remembered that story when I recently started interviewing real estate agents to sell The Manor. I was looking for sincerity and warmth, because I'd spent seventeen years caring for this house. My puppy, Madison, liked—no, loved— almost everyone, so I didn't know how effective she would be. But I thought it was worth a try. The real estate agent would be spending a lot of time showing my house. I wanted him or her to fit in.

At the beginning of every meeting, once everyone had settled in, I called my assistant and asked her to send in Madison.

Like clockwork, I would then hear footsteps on the marble floor—Madison running faster and faster down the hall as she got closer to the family room, where we were sitting.

Two agents were quite smart, and had really done their homework. One brought treats for Madison, so it was love at first sight. Another brought her a squeaky toy. I thought Madison would have gone anywhere with her. Those two were in like Flynn, as far as Madison was concerned.

It shouldn't have been hard for all the real estate agents to figure out I was a dog person. They'd all toured the house before we met, and my home is full of paintings of dogs, including my favorite, *I'se Biggest*, with the girl and her Saint

Bernard, and even an oil painting of dogs playing poker, which hangs prominently in Aaron's game room. We have statues of dogs, sculptures of dogs, topiaries shaped like dogs in the gardens, and even a dog grooming area of the laundry room, complete with adjustable table, sink, blow dryers, and the latest in products.

Of the remaining three real estate agents, Madison clearly didn't like two of the teams. One man was obviously not a dog person, so Madison wanted no part of him. I think he was relieved that Madison didn't want to be petted. I crossed him off the list.

Another agent was forcing himself to be friendly with Madison, but he was clearly uncomfortable. I didn't like his marketing plan anyway.

Look, everybody, look.

Listen to the dogs.

They know who's good and who's not.

At least with appraisers and Realtors.

Thank you, Annie.

Thank you, Madison.

Thank you, Spot.

And thank you, God, not only for creating dogs, but for your generosity in allowing *GOD* spelled backward to become *DOG*.

Chapter 8

Size Does Matter, Especially in Hollywood

Dick Powell's office was typical of big-shot digs. Once you entered, his desk was so far away that by the time you started walking toward the chair opposite his desk, he grew to be 15 feet tall and I shrunk to 15 inches.

My husband remembered that life-changing 1956 job interview in his autobiography, *Aaron Spelling: Prime-Time*

Life. When he told me the story years earlier, I told him my own impressions of offices and how they defined the man.

Ozzie Nelson didn't have one.

Jim Anderson's was really tiny, and seemed to have only a desk, one pen, and a coatrack.

Ward Cleaver shared his with Lumpy's father, and it was small.

Sheriff Andy Taylor not only shared his with his deputy, but the jail was right there, too.

Beverly Hillbillies banker Mr. Drysdale's was fairly large, but people were always charging in and disrupting his schemes.

Major and astronaut Anthony Nelson had an office that was big enough for a genie to pop in and out of all the time.

I realized that as likable and as good as these TV characters probably were, none was very successful. If they had been, they would have had much bigger offices.

It was going to be different when I had a successful husband. He'd have a big office.

I guess we succeeded. In a 1987 story, Stephen Farber of *The New York Times* alluded to Aaron Spelling's "enormous office" and said that Aaron referred to it as "my own 'Fantasy Island.'"

And then, of course, on-screen TV offices changed, thanks to my husband. Blake Carrington and Alexis Carrington Colby had "enormous" offices by television standards.

Of course, when I learned more about television, I realized

there was no point in characters in *Father Knows Best* or *The Beverly Hillbillies* having large offices, as it just would have wasted time to have the camera pan the office or make characters walk extra steps to get to their desks or phones.

One Hollywood office, however, stood above all others. From the minute I read my first movie magazine, I realized that the standard for all time for executive offices was the big office that belonged to little Louis B. Mayer.

When it came to exercising his power by intimidating people with his grandiosity, Mayer, co-founder of Metro-Goldwyn-Mayer, didn't seem to miss a trick.

My movie magazines recounted how when the stars were called to Mayer's office, they would have to pass beautiful cinema artifacts, scores of movie posters, five or six assistants scurrying about, and then finally arrive at the mammoth desk of diminutive Mr. Mayer. I envisioned the glamorous Greta Garbo and dashing Clark Gable, usually so self-assured, heading to Mayer's desk to ask for a raise or a favor and getting increasingly timid as they approached.

Now that was good mogul psychology. I knew I had to remember that for my future husband's own office—never dreaming, of course, that my future husband would become a Hollywood mogul himself.

I kept notes: Mayer's secretaries sat in an anteroom that could have passed for any successful executive's office. But that was just the entry hall. The office itself had mammoth walnut doors that opened to a completely white room. Sixty feet of white carpet transported visitors past white walls, under white ceilings, past white chairs and sofas. Touches of silver were everywhere, just to add some flash.

And then people would encounter Mr. Louis B. Mayer, all five-foot-five and 175 pounds of him, seated behind a white-leather-sided, crescent-shaped desk.

Wow! I knew no one was thinking, "He's really short." No, the image he projected was clear: "This is the most powerful man in show business."

When I learned that the president's office in the White House was less than thirty-six feet long and twenty-nine feet across, I appreciated Mayer even more. That man really knew how to make a statement. This showed in his movies, of course, including *The Wizard of Oz*, *Easter Parade*, and *Gone With the Wind*.

Over the years, whenever I visited an important person's office, I made mental notes. I tried not to judge the executive by the size of his office, but I could never get the image of Mayer's intimidating and daunting white office out of my mind.

Aaron and I both laughed about how much the size of an office colored our views of Hollywood and success. I made more and more notes, knowing they might be useful one day once my own mogul's empire had grown. As my husband's company became more successful, had more shows and movies, and added more and more staff, he always needed more space.

Finally, in the late 1970s, it was time to create the signature Aaron Spelling office. I didn't tell him that's what I was doing. I just said that I wanted him to have an office that would accommodate all his needs and staff.

He loved Hollywood, so of course he wanted an office in Hollywood. Over the years he'd had offices at 20th Century-Fox, ABC, and on Wilshire Boulevard's "Miracle Mile," but he wanted to be in Hollywood proper.

We found space at the historic Warner Hollywood studios, and took over the space where some of television's biggest successes had been produced. The offices previously housed Quinn Martin, whose QM Productions was responsible for *Streets of San Francisco*, *Barnaby Jones*, *Cannon*, *Twelve O'Clock High*, *The Fugitive*, *The FBI*, and others.

Warner Hollywood had many great Hollywood stories. In 1922 the newly built studio became the Pickford-Fairbanks Studios, the home of Mary Pickford and Douglas Fairbanks. Several years later the studio was renamed United Artists Studio, after Pickford and Fairbanks united with Charlie Chaplin, D. W. Griffith, and Samuel Goldwyn. In the late 1930s, Goldwyn renamed it again, and it became the Samuel Goldwyn Studios. Over the years, Fairbanks's *Robin Hood* and classics such as *Wuthering Heights*, *Guys and Dolls*, *The Best Years of Our Lives*, and *West Side Story* were shot there. Warner Bros. bought it, and the name became Warner Hollywood Studios just before Aaron moved in.

It was a perfect location. Aaron had built the amazing *Love Boat* set—complete with swimming pool and life-size exteriors and interiors of the ship itself—at Warner Hollywood, and a lot of *Dynasty* was shot on a sound stage on the lot.

The space already had a great legacy, and Aaron was going to continue its tradition. We didn't set out to top the last generation of moguls. We just wanted a space befitting a man who personified show business and where characters from Charlie and his Angels to the Carringtons and others from *Dynasty* would fit in; a place where the members of *The Mod Squad* would go to research the history of Hollywood for a case, or where Mr. Roarke could send an executive seeking the ultimate fantasy.

Let me walk you through it.

Guests would enter downstairs and then wait in a reception area and see the imposing AARON SPELLING PRODUCTIONS plaque. Very few of them saw the private dining room and other offices. The dining room was furnished in antiques, with a beautiful armoire and a buffet where we stored the china.

And then they would be escorted to Aaron's top assistant's office, and, *poof,* the Hollywood magic would happen.

The start of their journey to see Aaron began, with a flourish, when his assistant pushed a button and the off-center wooden doors to his office swung open. There, forty-eight feet away, was Aaron sitting in his high-backed leather padded chair at his huge desk.

It was a long walk to get to him. Even I felt like what Greta Garbo or Katharine Hepburn must have experienced walking toward Mayer, with every step, losing her confidence in getting whatever she was going to demand. Don't worry. I always regained my confidence. I'm sure Garbo and Hepburn got what they wanted, too.

I'm not sure how we arrived at the distance of forty-eight feet. It was definitely a smaller space than Louis B. Mayer had, although larger than the Oval Office. But ours wasn't taxpayer-supported, so we could spend whatever we wanted without having to worry about voters wondering how their taxes were being spent.

If you're like me and not good at numbers, forty-eight feet is the height of the Garfield balloon in the Macy's Thanksgiving Day Parade. Each of the giant steel letters in the famous Hollywood sign is forty-five feet tall. The distance from Aaron's office entrance to his desk was three times the length of Lady Liberty's hand and a few inches longer than her right arm. Each column in the Lincoln Memorial is forty-four feet. Lindbergh's *Spirit of St. Louis*, which in 1927 took him across the Atlantic Ocean for the first time, had a forty-six-foot wingspan. (I saw the plane at the Smithsonian National Air and Space Museum later; forty-six feet is quite a distance.) The wingspan of the Wright Brothers' 1902 *Wright Flyer* was just over forty feet.

Forty-eight feet is a long, long way.

As a visitor made his way across the room, to the right was a fireplace and the door to Aaron's private dressing room and bathroom. Farther down were a game table and four chairs, where Aaron sometimes ate during a lunch meeting. Oh, yes, and he had a butler to escort people to their seats and make sure they had whatever they wanted to eat or drink.

To the left was a beautiful twenty-four-foot-long four-piece sectional sofa, upholstered in beige silk. Three large square coffee tables sat in front of the sofas. Bookcases were everywhere, and some of Aaron's memorabilia and awards were spread out tastefully. His television was built into the bookcase wall. Everything was large.

The walls were all upholstered in raw silk, to match the sofa. The carpeting was custom-made deep pile wool in a wave design in two tones of beige. Cashmere throws were carefully placed.

The same assistant who controlled the automatic doors was in charge of inspecting the carpet after every meeting. "Spot on the rug" was the phrase everyone—except the rug cleaners and makers of spot removers—dreaded.

If there was to be an official conference, rather than a regular meeting, giant round-back swivel chairs would be moved to the other side of the coffee tables.

Aaron always had a pipe in his mouth, and his desk had pipe holders and pipe supplies we had collected from all over the world. The pipes were much more prominent even than his TV mogul trappings of scripts, notes, and head shots.

Behind his desk was a delicate English antique table, a contrast to the big heavy desk, which displayed his favorite photos of me and our children. Some People's Choice and other awards were placed among the photos. We both liked everything to be in its place, and neither of us would leave his office without making sure everything was exactly where it should be.

Just for Aaron, and rarely noticed until people were leaving, was a floor-to-ceiling bubbled fish tank, installed to catch Aaron's eye when he sat at his desk. He found it relaxing, and I was so happy when I'd see him watching the fascinating and graceful puffer fish, clown fish, and tiger fish as a temporary diversion from the pressures of running Hollywood's largest and most successful production company. The tank relaxed him so much that we duplicated it at home.

Aaron's new headquarters had "Hollywood" written all over it.

I think it worked—maybe a little too well.

Our feelings were hurt when a *Los Angeles Times* reporter described Aaron's office as "gargantuan." That was not an Aaron and Candy word. *Glamorous* would have been nice. *Extravagant* might have stung a little but it would have been appropriate. But not *gargantuan*.

It was somewhere between Dick Powell and Louis B. Mayer.

Aaron's desk was a combination of beautiful and imposing dark wood, probably ten feet across, with intricate designs carved into it. I still love that desk; when he retired, we moved it to his office at The Manor. It still sits there, basking in the sun from the gardens outside, and overlooking the scripts covering the thousands of hours of entertainment Aaron produced.

Aaron's office was, in a word, spectacular. Guests felt important, and they knew they were dealing with an important executive. That was the idea, and it worked. By the way, Aaron was five foot eleven, so we weren't trying to camouflage anything.

I'm not sure what we would do if we were faced with constructing a new office for a mogul today. Times have changed dramatically in the past two decades. Some of the Hollywood talent agencies are still building giant buildings, aimed to set records, and I know they need to distinguish themselves.

Aaron was already distinguished, and his office wasn't built to set records. In fact, his record success enabled us to create and build the exquisite office.

Today, in our online and virtual world, though, maybe we could have saved a lot of money and just bought him a Microsoft Office suite.

Aaron, of course, wouldn't have wanted the standard or small business versions. Even the professional version wouldn't have been enough. But now people can buy their own servers, and there's even an "Ultimate Office" program.

With all the technology, Aaron would have needed fewer assistants. The mailroom could have been practically eliminated. He could probably have done his own titles and graphics with some of the software. Script changes could easily have been made online. He could have watched the dailies on his laptop. He wouldn't have wanted to, but he could have done his own spreadsheets, contact lists, and photocopies.

And he could have worked at home all the time and used the butler and chef who already worked at the house.

On second thought, I think he'd still have gone for the big office on the lot, with his assistants, his own butler and chef, and even the postage meter and giant copy machines.

Aaron liked being a mogul. I liked that he could have the trappings. It worked. From that office came *Beverly Hills 90210*, *Melrose Place*, *Charmed*, and *Seventh Heaven*.

And he really did have his own richly deserved *Fantasy Island* in the middle of old Hollywood.

Chapter 9

✤

Wizards and Showgirls Need Fifty-Two Suitcases

When your husband doesn't fly and is hesitant to take time off from work, you want to make sure the monthlong vacation he agrees to take with the family is perfect.

The year was 1984. Tori was ten, and Randy was five. Aaron had *Dynasty, The Love Boat, Fantasy Island, Matt Houston, T. J. Hooker, Hotel,* and the miniseries *Hollywood Wives* in production; and I was, as always, behind the scenes, helping him with everything from policies to presents for his company of sixteen hundred employees, making his world mogul-like, and striving to be the best mother in the history of motherhood.

Our vacations had been simple and routine. When the kids were growing up we would go to the beach almost every weekend and spend time together there. "Time away" was usually the five-hour drive to Las Vegas, or two hours to Palm Springs. One time, when Tori was four, we took a *Love Boat* cruise. She wanted to spend all her time in the casino.

Once, when we were getting ready for a cruise to England, we reminded Tori of that earlier cruise. Her father wanted to know if she remembered the security guards telling her she had to stop playing the slot machines because she was too young.

"I have a confession to make," Aaron told Tori. "I told them you were a midget and that they were insulting you. They left you alone after that, and you kept pumping dimes into the slot machines."

As I prepared, I kept thinking it didn't seem that long ago that we were borrowing suitcases from the set of *Hotel* to take on a family vacation. Those trips to Las Vegas—Aaron drove and I flew to make sure everything was right when he arrived—were, I hoped, good practice for this once-in-a-lifetime family adventure.

There was no rehearsal. There would be no encore. This was to be an epic Hollywood-style Spelling Family Vacation that wouldn't be duplicated, imitated, or properly captured.

Our experiences were part Auntie Mame, introducing her nephew, Patrick, to the wonders of the world, samples of Lucy and Ricky's European misadventures, flashes of Grace Kelly being wined and dined by Prince Rainier, and one of the best times our family ever had as we shared so many once-in-a-lifetime experiences together. We were hosted and entertained in a manner beyond description. Ah, showbiz perks.

In 1984, Aaron Spelling's shows accounted for one third of ABC-TV's prime-time schedule. That made us really, really, really, really important to the network, and so many people went out of their way to make sure we were happy, entertained, and felt really, really, really important. We were, and we did.

We used every mode of transportation except an airplane.

That meant we had to start with a private railroad car to get us from Los Angeles to New York. Some people saw the U.S.A. in their Chevrolet. We saw the country from the luxury of a private train car, the *Cannonball*, a vintage 1929 train from Brownsville, Texas, hitched to the back of an Amtrak train. Another car was added for our fifty-two pieces of luggage. More on that later.

I learned a lot about train rules and regulations, train furniture, train food, sleeping arrangements on trains, and how to keep children amused on long train rides. I found a new appreciation of our beautiful country as the train traveled through small towns and skirted big cities, and was reminded how far from mainstream America we lived. Looking out the windows, we said, maybe, when Aaron retired, we'd move to the country. We knew we wouldn't.

Our *Cannonball* had beautiful wood décor and touches not found on modern train cars. It wasn't our first choice, as we'd wanted something modern. But we found out we'd have to switch railroads in order to tow our car from Union Pacific to Penn Central, and propane tanks were forbidden on those routes. So, after much research, we found the 1929 car with a wood-burning stove that would be our home for a few days before and after Europe. It sounded better than it was. Everything smelled as though it had been barbecued with wood chips. Aaron and I were so self-conscious when we dressed up in a gown and tux for a European dinner or party and brought the smell of the American Southwest with us. No one asked. We didn't tell. We wondered if the odor lingered after we left a room, but were too embarrassed to ask any of our hosts.

The train car was a marvel to behold. I never saw so many things fold up and expand to turn into other useful things. We ate dinner at a table that converted to bunk beds. Our kitchen counter became a makeshift shower. Straps appeared everywhere to keep us in our beds at night, when the train went faster.

I've never been a good sleeper, but this was among the most difficult times I've ever had. I brought some of my favorite sheets from home, knowing in advance I'd need all the help I could get to feel comfortable. They didn't make a dent. I felt every bump, every turn, every movement of the straps touching my skin. Aaron said I was like his very own "princess and the pea." I was not amused, just tired.

I had arranged for one of our television sets to be put on the train, so Randy could play his favorite Coleco video games during the day. We had board games, cards, and other amusements, too. Fortunately, I also brought some video-tapes, which were my salvation at night when I couldn't sleep, and the kids could watch their movies all day. Even though my entire family was sleeping within feet of the tel-evision, none of them shared my misery. I watched movies and got crabby. They slept soundly. The video boxes smelled like burnt wood.

I bought Aaron a diary with a blue velvet cover and a gold plate that read, THE SPELLINGS EUROPE 1984, and asked him to keep a journal with what I knew would be his unique view of our family vacation.

The only rule was that he had to promise not to refer to us as the Von Trapp Family. One of our security guards said we looked like the family fleeing Austria in *The Sound of Music*. I said we were having a good time and didn't want to be compared to wartime refugees. I also gave Tori and Randy diaries. They were bored by the time we got to Phoenix.

I'll let Aaron help me narrate our trip.

June 27 journal entry:

> *Arrived at Union Station to the biggest surprise of our*
> *lives . . . photographers, friends and fantastic party.*
> *It was a miniature trip of New York, Paris and Lon-*
> *don with food, dress extras and music to match. It*
> *was by far the most spectacular sendoff one could*
> *imagine.*
>
> *The emotional moment happened as we stood on*
> *the observation deck of our private car and waved*
> *goodbye. Candy and I were crying, but they were tears*
> *of happiness.*

June 28:

> *Short stop at Flagstaff, Arizona. We got off for three*
> *minutes. Why? Because it was there and someone had*
> *to do it.*

He also reported that we got off the train in Albuquerque
to buy a few loaves of white bread because we wanted white
bread and the train didn't stock it.

> *So far, I haven't read one script or called the studio.*
> *Now we have a ninth wonder of the world.*

June 29:

> *Stopped in Chicago for three hour layover. We piled*
> *into a limousine and headed for Marshall Fields.*

When we got back to the station, the train was late. We spent over an hour in an arcade at the station, watching the kids play Pac-Man. It's as if we never left home!

June 30:

Arrived in New York and went to the Pierre Hotel, only to find one of our bags had vanished. All of Randy's underwear was gone. Oh, well, the hazards of traveling.

Thank God they had a maid waiting to unpack for Candy. So far, it's the best thing that's happened to her on the trip.

He was right. White bread in Albuquerque and a rushed trip to a department store weren't highlights. Now, if they had let me play Pac-Man with them, that could have been good family fun. By the way, I have two Pac-Man games in my house, Pac-Man and Ms. Pac-Man, and I do frequently play them.

July 1:

We all went to Bloomingdale's to buy the things Randy lost. We thought it would take about an hour. Two-and-a-half hours later, the store had closed—and we were still there.

Long story short: It took a long time to get someone to approve our check, and we went through all our secret hiding places to find enough cash. It then took more than an hour to write up our purchases.

Aaron continued:

> *It was the pits. Candy and I may never speak to Betsy Bloomingdale again.*

We do. Sorry, Betsy.

The next day, we visited with executives at ABC. Then Aaron had a press conference for about forty magazine and newspaper reporters, who normally didn't get to see him. That night, we surprised *La Cage Aux Folles* star Gene Barry backstage after the show on Broadway (Gene had starred in Aaron's *Burke's Law* series), went to the Plaza, ate at 21, and had what Aaron called "a very exciting hectic day."

July 3:

> *A day of sight-seeing starting at FAO Schwarz for the kids. It took three hours to get out of there.*

Yes, we shopped across country (and the continent). We ended that shopping day when Tori wanted a T-shirt that read, I LOVE N.Y. Randy, who wasn't a big fan of shopping—especially now that he had underwear again—said he wanted one that said, I HATE N.Y. We never found one.

We spent July 4 on a yacht going to Ellis Island and the Statue of Liberty. Aaron continued in his journal:

> *There were surprises galore. First, they [ABC] had the Goodyear Blimp fly so close to our boat that it was scary. ABC had it flown in from Washington. Then Mayor Koch came by on a police boat to wave hello. Then a helicopter flew around us for ten minutes as its light spelled out, "Welcome Candy, Aaron, Tori and Randy from your friends at ABC. Bon Voyage!"*

July 5:

> *Left for Washington on our train car. Trip was marvelous. We went to the Smithsonian Institute to see the airplane exhibit. Breathtaking. Later piled in the limo to see all the monuments lit up at night. We passed the White House. Just think, tomorrow we'll be inside of it. I feel like a real American tourist— and I like the feeling.*

We didn't feel "regular" for long. Here's Aaron's account for July 6:

> *Arrive at the White House at 11 a.m., through security at 11:30. We went to the upstairs (just Candy and me) where we were met by the First Lady. Nancy took us to her private sitting room for coffee.*

We were told that Nancy was rushed because it was her birthday, so she could only see us for half an hour. Well, she kept us for over an hour and then surprised us by sending for the kids and a photographer. Tori was a little princess. She did a lovely curtsy and said, "Hello, Mrs. Reagan." Randy made a lovely bow and said, "Hello, Mrs. President." Nancy broke up. She took us to the Oval Office, Ronnie's study and Lincoln Bedroom. What a lady! No wonder she's first!

Later, we all had lunch in the White House mess and toured the lower part of the mansion. We were then whisked off for a special guided tour of the Capitol building. My biggest thrill was the House of Representatives.

What a day. I've never felt prouder to be an American. What the hell is a little Jewish kid from Texas doing in the White House????

That was my Aaron. I felt the same way. Our kids? Well, it wasn't easy keeping them humble.

I feel the need to reveal a secret I've kept for twenty-five years. We let Randy jump on the bed in the Lincoln Bedroom. I'm sorry, Nancy.

We had known the Reagans before they moved to Washington, and they were lovely people. We really felt at home in the White House, but we were very nervous.

Randy wanted cinnamon toast, and Nancy was happy to oblige. Aaron and I knew better than to take any because we didn't want to leave crumbs. Our son didn't worry about mundane things like dropping crumbs in the White House. The sight I will never forget was of Aaron trailing his handsome son in his little suit and, literally, picking up crumbs from the hallways and the Lincoln Bedroom. I was laughing at Aaron when we heard our son say, "Mrs. President, you serve the best cinnamon toast I've ever tasted."

We later ate club sandwiches with Nancy, and neither of us left any crumbs behind.

On July 8 we got on the *QEII* to begin our journey to Europe. Aaron and I had a suite unlike any stateroom on *The Love Boat*. It was the Queen Elizabeth Suite, which Aaron termed "gorgeous," even though that wasn't an Aaron word. The fixtures and furniture were beautifully classic, but not the opulence we later saw in the film *Titanic*. In fact, the *Orient Express*, which we boarded after we landed, was far more elegant. Our stateroom was large and very comfortable and had a big round beige sofa outside our bedroom, where we would relax after a day of walking around the ship.

After all those years of Aaron producing *Love Boat*, you'd think we'd know our way around a cruise ship. No. We knew our way around the set in Hollywood, but the *QEII* was something else.

Actually, let me correct that. Aaron wrote,

> *The ship is so big that I am totally lost. The only one*
> *who seems to know where everything is—you've got*
> *it—is Tori.*

As the ship left New York, we passed the Statue of Liberty. Aaron got emotional, remembering that his last time doing so was on a troop ship during World War II.

On July 9, Aaron wrote that Nelia, one of the nannies, was seasick and the doctor was giving her a shot.

> *We toured the ship and all the shops, but Candy*
> *didn't buy anything. I hope she's not sick, too.*

I wasn't.

It was an amazing cruise. We dressed for dinner: Tori in a long gown, and Randy in a tux. "They're adorable," Aaron wrote. "Candy and I are very proud."

By July 11, Aaron was writing on Post-it notes instead of in his journal. Was the thrill gone?

> *Heard about dock strike.*
> *Lost at Bingo.*
> *Tori won prize for doing movie.*
> *Randy learned about sinking of Titanic.*

Leaving downtown L.A. to catch our train to Europe in 1984. *(Spelling Family Archives)*

"My Will"

When I die from eating a worm I leave all my po-seshoms to my family: my Mom, pop, & Brother Morgen.

To My Mom I will leave ⅓ of my astate, & to my pop I leave ⅓ ed of my astate & to my brother I leave ⅓ ed of my estate which is $30.00, and allso I leave my dog morgen ta my Mom and to morgen he will get the rest of my poseshons

(over)

which what ever they may be;

Signature
Candy Moores

195**

"My Will" in 1954 when I thought I was dying from eating half a worm in my artichoke. *(Spelling Family Archives)*

Small wedding, big cake, and enormous happiness in 1968. (*Spelling Family Archives*)

Aaron admitted to Hollywood columnist Harrison Carroll that he wanted to marry me! I kept the 1966 clipping.

A "candid" shot as we left the party at Rock Hudson's house in 1966. (*Spelling Family Archives*)

(Sigh) Rock Hudson, my husband-to-be-I-fantasized when I was eight. (© *Bettmann/CORBIS*)

At home with *Dynasty* star John Forsythe and Prince Rainier of Monaco. *(Spelling Family Archives)*

My sweet husband always said he loved my cooking. I worried that he was so thin when we married in 1968. *(Spelling Family Archives)*

I was thrilled to meet designer Halston. *(Spelling Family Archives)*

Modeling a bikini at age eighteen. The photographer told me to look "confident." *(Spelling Family Archives)*

I took my first official modeling shots while I was still in high school. *(Spelling Family Archives)*

I was asked to model jewelry for fashion magazines, and we added a touch of *Dynasty*. *(Spelling Family Archives)*

Aaron invited me to the set of *The Mod Squad*. We're pictured with costar Clarence Williams III. *(Spelling Family Archives)*

A family night
out with Randy,
Aaron, and Tori
in 2001. *(Spelling
Family Archives)*

The Manor decorated for
Christmas 2007. *(Amir Kojoory)*

Snow in our backyard for the kids
at Christmas? Why not? *(Spelling
Family Archives)*

Aaron surprised me with a party to
renew our vows on our sixteenth
wedding anniversary. We alternated
dancing with each other and Tori
and Randy all night. *(Spelling Family
Archives)*

We had two children and four dogs, so why leave home? *(Spelling Family Archives)*

Aaron, Tori, Siegfried, Randy, Candy, and Roy, backstage after the Siegfried and Roy show in Las Vegas. *(Spelling Family Archives)*

There's my wheaten terrier, Madison, at home, age eight months, in summer 2008. *(Spelling Family Archives)*

Randy asked, "Mom, you didn't really bake a birthday cake for the dog, did you?" I did. *(Spelling Family Archives)*

memo from

Aaron Spelling

What is a Valentine?
A care?
A love?
A belief?
If it is all or any of
these things,
Then you truly are my
Valentine. Much love,

H.

Aaron was a great writer, even of casual love notes. *(Spelling Family Archives)*

THOMAS / SPELLING PRODUCTIONS

Danny Thomas
Aaron Spelling

HOLLYWOOD 9-5911
846 NORTH CAHUENGA BOULEVARD
HOLLYWOOD, CALIFORNIA 90038

Dearest Candy:

Happy Anniversary! One week right now ---- and they said it wouldn't last!

I love you,

H.

P.S. You're adorable.

P.P.S. I'm very proud of you.

P.P.P.S. I love you very much.

P.P.P.P.S. I know I've told you these things before, but you're going to hear them every anniversary$$

ABOVE: Friends decorated our *Cannonball* train car with a "Bon Voyage" banner. *(Spelling Family Archives)*

RIGHT: Saying good-bye to friends at the station as the train left Los Angeles for our European adventure. *(Spelling Family Archives)*

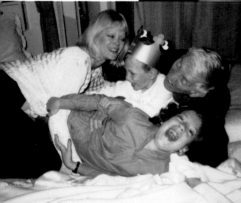

Yes, I encouraged my kids to jump on beds, as long as they didn't do it at home. *(Spelling Family Archives)*

Randy bowed to Nancy Reagan during our White House tour and said, "Hello, Mrs. President." *(Official White House photograph)*

My mid-1960s look for a winter modeling catalog. *(Spelling Family Archives)*

Barbara Stanwyck was a great friend and godmother to Tori and Randy.
(Spelling Family Archives)

I hit the "Top Dollar" jackpot in Las Vegas and won $100,000 in 2007. *(Spelling Family Archives)*

With Mom and Dad at my Sweet Sixteen. *(Spelling Family Archives)*

TOP ROW: J. Goldstein, Miss Pyle, B. Bloomfield, S. Siskin, Miss McClure, D. Hannam, H. Rosene. BOTTOM ROW: B. Shapiro, A. Ehrnstein, C. Marer, C. Speigal, P. Kotz, E. Halbreich.

HOME
ECONOMICS
CLUB

Our high school Home Economics Club in 1962 really cooked. *(Spelling Family Archives)*

Any girl interested in Home Economics was eligible to join this club. Some of their activities were candy sales, sending packages and letters to families of other countries, and organizing social affairs such as teas, dinners, and punch parties. This organization provided its members with excellent training for a future in homemaking.

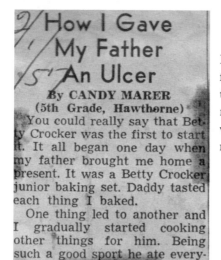

How I Gave My Father An Ulcer

By CANDY MARER
(5th Grade, Hawthorne)

You could really say that Betty Crocker was the first to start it. It all began one day when my father brought me home a present. It was a Betty Crocker junior baking set. Daddy tasted each thing I baked.

One thing led to another and I gradually started cooking other things for him. Being such a good sport he ate everything I cooked; and now, I think, poor Dad has an ulcer.

In 1957, I was terrified I gave my father an ulcer with food I made with the Betty Crocker baking set he gave me. I wrote him an apology letter, which my parents sent to our local newspaper. *(Spelling Family Archives)*

My monkey bread recipe. *(Spelling Family Archives)*

§ Monkey Bread   oven 400°

1) Soften 2 cakes yeast in 1/4 c. warm water. Add 1/4 c. ev. sugar (1/2 c. Sugar not 1/4)

2) Scald 1 c. milk and put in big mixing bowl. add 1/2 c. (1 cube) butter, 1 t. salt and 3 beaten eggs cool to lukewarm, Then add yeast mixture

3) Add 3 or 4 c. flour, beating well until soft dough is formed. Knead until smooth

4) allow to rise until doubled in bulk. Roll 1/4 in thick, Spread with melted butter cut in dimonds and arrange in greased ring mold. Let double in size. Bake 45 min or until brown
greased ring mold. Let double in size. Bake 45 min or until brown

Candy's Dynasty

It's not easy to escape her famous last name. Candy Spelling is the wife of prolific television producer Aaron Spelling, the man who has brought us such prime-time hits as *The Mod Squad, The Love Boat, Charlie's Angels, Fantasy Island* and *Beverly Hills, 90210*. On the latter program, a Wednesday-night viewing staple for teenagers around the world, Spelling's daughter, Tori, has made a name for herself as a talented, believable actress portraying sensitive, good-hearted Donna.

Myths and legends have surrounded Spelling's life, and so it's quite fitting that her first dolls from Knickerbocker are the Fantasy Dolls line. The Follow Me From A to Z series is an excursion through the alphabet, where the phonetics of spelling come to three-dimensional life. We see how "A" is for apple, and "B" is for bird and "C" is for clock. You get the picture—doll collecting as a fun, hands-on flash card. Sculpted by celebrated doll artist Sandra Bilotto, these eight-inch vinyl characters are instructional and well crafted. "I wanted these to be vinyl so that children are able to touch the clothing and feel the faces," Spelling asserts. "There are some dolls that you want to put up

high on the shelf so that they can't be handled. But if you make all dolls unaccessible, where will the future collectors come from?"

As a tribute to adult collectors, Spelling has collaborated, once again, with Bilotto to fashion Jewelie. The doll with the unique spelling is a tribute to Candy's husband ("The name 'Julie' has always been a good-luck charm for him. He's always had a hit when there was a Julie in his shows."), as well as an homage to her own fascination with hunting "splendid mementos" and gathering "fabulous jewelry."

Jewelie is a vinyl 17-inch fashion doll who represents a well-dressed world traveler. As she scours the globe looking for fine paintings

Elementary, my dear Watson! You needn't be a sleuth to realize that Candy Spelling's Follow Me From A to Z provides fun ways to learn. These eight-inch vinyl dolls are designed by Spelling and sculpted by Sandra Bilotto. "E" is for Eskimo, at left, and "F" is for fruit, above, are $57 and $55, respectively.

and glittering gems, the doll will be made available in breathtaking costumes accompanied by her latest sought-after treasures. Carmen Sandiego has nothing on this frequent flier!

"I was thrilled to work on these,"

Who's that stunning gal sampling the night life and perusing the art scene? It's Jewelie, one of Candy Spelling's Fantasy Dolls. With the allure of a mod angel, this 17-inch vinyl fashion doll is a beautiful brunette collector. She travels the globe and brings back souvenir-charms. She and her marvelous mementos are $129.

Spelling says in her clear, warm voice. "I've always loved to design clothing and jewelry for myself, and now I get to share that love with you. It's like a dream come true!" Incidentally, a portion of the sales of Candy Spelling's dolls will go to the Centro de Niños, one of her special charities. **—SF**

A magazine story called "Candy's Dynasty" about the dolls I created and sold on QVC in 1990.

Some of our luggage en route to the *Cannonball. (Spelling Family Archives)*

My grandmother Helen, brother Tony, Mom, Dad, and me in 1958.
(Spelling Family Archives)

Me as a high school senior, thinking I was ready to face the world, but not quite prepared to be married just weeks after graduation.
(Spelling Family Archives)

Tori wanted an "I Love NY" shirt. Randy wanted "I Hate NY," but settled for "love."
(Spelling Family Archives)

The poem "To My Mother" made my birthday in 1996 very special when twenty-three-year-old Tori lovingly gave me her beautifully framed words and pictures. Aaron and I treasured it, displayed it prominently, and even used it to comfort each other when Tori later started to say negative things about our family. I wanted to share it in my book, but out of respect to Tori, I have asked the publisher to keep some of her sentiments private. *(Spelling Family Archives)*

To
My
Mother ❤️...

You've been the greatest blessing
in my life, it's clear to me.

I'm glad you're My Mother..
I'm glad you're My friend!

I ❤️ U
Tori
xoxo
9/20/96

I almost caused a chain reaction crash on busy La Cienega Boulevard when I drove by and saw our names in a store window display. *(Spelling Family Archives)*

And, on the same Post-it, on July 12:

Costumes all—Tori as showgirl; Randy as wizard.
Both won prizes.
Hectic day—lots of worrying about strike.

We docked on July 13, but in Cherbourne, not London, because of the strike. Aaron summed up his Post-it note with: "Champagne, flowers, etc., everywhere."

ABC had arranged for an airplane to take us the short distance to our destination in London. But nope, Aaron didn't even take short flights when dock strikes disrupted plans. We ended up on a hovercraft, which turned out to be a fun adventure. The kids loved it because none of their friends had ever ridden in a hovercraft, as least as far as any of us knew. They couldn't wait to go home to tell everyone. But we told them we'd only just begun.

Day after day, we did one incredible thing after another. Watching the kids enjoy the experiences, sights, and sounds was the best. They weren't as impressed as we were with the fine restaurants, but they certainly loved hearing the stories and seeing the Tower of London, Buckingham Palace, the changing of the guard, Westminster Abbey, Trafalgar Square (where they fed the pigeons), and the statues of war heroes—and yes, going shopping.

On our last day in London, Aaron noted: "Went to Jacobs and bought two automobiles."

It's not what it sounds like. Yes, we bought a London checker cab and a red Ferrari, but they weren't for us. The Jacobs showroom with the miniature motorized cars in the window was near our hotel, the Dorchester, and no matter where we were walking, the kids steered us toward the showroom. Tori begged for one, then two, cars. Randy joined in. No matter where we were, the kids wanted to go back and look at the cars. Tori agonized over whether she wanted the Ferrari or the Mercedes more. Randy wanted the yellow checkered cab with black writing.

Aaron's journal revealed the bottom line: We weren't good at saying "no" to Randy and Tori. We bought them the cars and arranged for them to be shipped home. They took months to get to California, as Tori and Randy reminded us almost every day when one of them would say something like, "I feel like taking a drive today." They did enjoy them, and we did enjoy watching them driving around our property in their European imports.

Aaron's Post-it notes ended, and the rest of his parchment pages remained empty, except for one last one:

Bought great crystal cabinet at Goode's.
Bought piece of luggage to add to our other 49 pieces.

Wizards and Showgirls Need Fifty-Two Suitcases

Tori and Randy went to Windsor Castle to see the Queen's Doll Castle.

Candy packed the rest of the day.

Then, we took the *Orient Express* back to France.

As I write this, it's still hard to believe. We visited the Louvre; toured Versailles as a guest of the Duc d'Orleans; went to Chanel, where Aaron picked out beautiful outfits for me; bought clothes for Randy and Tori at La Foyette; splurged on matching Vacheron Constantin watches (and now I wear his, which has a bigger face), and I hoped we could return there one day. We also bought a Cartier mystery clock, which we decided would always remind us of the wonderful vacation our family enjoyed.

The trip continued for two more weeks as we reversed our elegant trip across the Atlantic and boarded our train car and returned home. We had almost forgotten about the wood smell, but the first night on our *Cannonball*, it returned.

In a life of biggers and betters, excesses and too muches, our family trip to Europe stands out as one of the highlights of any life. It wasn't about just the best hotels, limos, and yachts, the finest food and VIP tours. It was about sharing that month together, as a family; and in our kids' frame of reference, the trip was like the rest of their lives: with only the biggest and the best. It was difficult to make them understand that big-city mayors don't wave to everyone from police boats, and that most families are not welcomed with helicopters trailing banners or greeted by the First Lady in the private White House quarters. They knew their father worked in television and was important, but none of us could have conceived of how many people tried so hard to "VIP" us.

Aaron was wrong, by the way. As good a correspondent as he was, it was the fifty-third piece of luggage that we bought in England. Think about it. When you're dressing your kids as wizards and showgirls for dinners at sea, you really have to pack a lot.

I still have that luggage in my attic, and I never walk by it without smiling as I think of the happy memories of our family vacation in Europe. We never did take another family train trip. How could we top the first?

Chapter 10

1984 Was a Very Good Year, After All

I love horror movies.

The first one I remember was *House of Wax,* which came out when I was seven. I knew something was up when my brother, who was well on his way to teenage mischief by then, told my parents that the movie was a love story. Even then I wondered why he wanted us to go see a love story when there were a lot of Westerns out. It was even stranger when they handed out 3D glasses, but I put mine on to see love up close.

It wasn't a love story, but I fell in love that night with scary horror movies.

For those who don't love horror (and that's most of the people I know), *House of Wax* was one of those Vincent-Price-at-his-worst movies. Although I didn't understand why someone would want to set fire to his own wax museum, I did realize someone had done something really bad, and the scenes of people melting like wax stayed with me for a long time.

Anyway, dead bodies had started disappearing from the morgue (a word I think I first heard on *Dragnet*, but I wasn't sure). There was a lot of darkness and scary music, and this crazy guy wanted to make some girl into a wax figure of Marie Antoinette. At the time I didn't know who she was, but later I made some dolls which I dressed like her. It was also my first time hearing the word *guillotine* (I never learned how to spell it, though, or had an occasion to use one). Blood was everywhere, people screamed; my mother couldn't look.

My parents were horrified, my brother smirked, and I couldn't wait until the next monster was ready to hit theaters to scare me.

To digress, when I saw that Paris Hilton was going to be in the 2005 remake of the film and that it wasn't going to be in 3D, I decided I didn't have to see it. I was very attached to my 3D glasses, and they were part of my original experience. Nope, a remake wasn't necessary, and I wanted to keep my first memory of *House of Wax*.

The irony that *House of Wax* was my introduction to horror made itself clear years later. The movie co-starred Carolyn Jones, who married Aaron Spelling in 1953. So, while I was a preteen being frightened by Carolyn Jones in 3D horror, my husband-to-be was enjoying his new bride's big-screen success.

Anyway, my life of horror films had begun. My attic, filled with beautiful Christmas decorations and patriotic Independence Day symbols, also has a section for Halloween. Over the years, I've collected some of the worst examples of witches with scary laughs, bloody creatures who lunge toward unsuspecting visitors, and enough devil and skeleton costumes to outfit an elementary school.

I can't wait until the 99 Cents store, Costco, Bed, Bath & Beyond, and Target all get their Halloween decorations on the shelves. There's always something cheap and tacky there that I don't own yet. As soon as the calendar turns to October, severed hands; cookie jars in the shape of pumpkins; dog toys that look like bloody body parts; and Bela Lugosi, Boris Karloff, and Vincent Price lookalikes are strategically placed around my antiques and furniture. Dracula actually looks comfortable next to my fragile antique fans.

My favorite movie of all time is *Scanners*, the 1981 film known to most people as "the one where people's heads explode." In 1981, my kids were seven and two. I loved being their mother and Aaron's wife. Every minute of the day was taken up with household and business chores. And yet I somehow found the time to see *Scanners* five or six times when it first opened.

I don't know what the appeal was. I remember one review that said the special effects were "uproariously revolting."

The story concerns a prescription drug that creates unwitting "Scanners," or people who can read others' thoughts, invade their memories, and cause strangers' noses to bleed and other involuntary reactions. As more heads start exploding, the government, of course, gets involved. An all-out war between Scanners and non-Scanners erupts, with blood, gore, and horror. Boy, I like that movie.

I like fantasy, too, and that goes back to my liking to tell stories about characters in my collections or paintings or my dreams.

Turnabout was a 1940 movie that I must have seen for the first time on TV in the early 1960s. It is one of those old black-and-white movies with fuzzy sound, and it reminds me of *Topper*. I could never get enough of *Topper,* one of my favorite movies and TV series, because people got to do the impossible, like becoming invisible and watching and laughing at others. And the dog drank martinis!

Turnabout is about a married couple who are bored with life and each other. Each thinks the other has a much better and more interesting life, and they wish they could trade places. Guess what! In the best tradition of later movies such as *Freaky Friday* and *Big*, and, with a puff of smoke, everything turns upside down, and there are laughs and lessons for all.

I still remember scenes from this hysterically funny movie, when a statue the couple receives as a wedding present wakes up and exchanges the personalities of the husband and the wife. The next morning, the gender-confused couple exchanges clothes and schedules and heads out into their new lives. She dons a man's business suit. He puts on what he calls a "frilly frock." And so it goes, with complications, mix-ups, and fun. I remember reading later that the film was classified as a "screwball comedy." That seemed to fit.

Of all of my husband's shows—and, yes, I dutifully watched every episode of every series, often multiple times, even though I had read the scripts already—my favorite was *Fantasy Island*. Aaron really liked that one, too.

The title was deceiving because people expected a wish-granting scenario where their wish would be Mr. Roarke's command.

What I liked about it was that it showed that there's no free ride. People would arrive at beautiful and seemingly carefree Fantasy Island to get their fantasies fulfilled, and impeccably white-suited Mr. Roarke would use superpowers to make them happy. But as in real life, the story showed that there are no real fantasies without consequences. Important life experiences were brought home as "Da plane! Da plane!" departed each week, and we were all a bit wiser.

Be careful what you wish for. Life doesn't always have happy endings, not even on TV.

I had my own movie fantasies, and they were named Cary Grant and Fred Astaire.

I used to have a dream, and it seemed to last for years: A prince on a white horse used to come to get me. He was supposed to take me to love and happiness ever after. It was a wonderful dream. But it never ended. We never left my bedroom or arrived at our destination.

I wanted to finish the dream and start my life with the prince. So, every night before I went to bed, I would write down where the dream had left off the night before, so my dream mechanism would know where to start. Sometimes I'd give myself hints, adding in parts of stories about Zorro, Cinderella, and Don Juan. My added inspirational suggestions didn't help. My prince arrived, and then . . .

As for Cary Grant, I wanted him to teach me all about being the womanly version of his kind of suave, so I could become the kind of woman he would want to date. I wanted him to take me in his arms, tell me smart things, give me that smile.

Fred Astaire was the other man of my dreams (not counting the prince on the white horse). I wanted to be one of the women who danced with him and who could brag that she'd done it backward and in high heels. I wanted him to take off his top hat when I walked into the room and sweep me into his arms. Astaire could sing *and* dance. I wonder if girls today feel that way about Justin Timberlake or Zac Efron.

Fade to 1989, when Aaron and I decided to give a big New Year's Eve party for our friends and co-workers. Our guest list looked like a Hollywood fantasy. I cautioned myself to remember *Fantasy Island* and what nasty surprises might be waiting for us.

There weren't any nasty surprises. It was another fantasy night in the life of the Spelling family and our friends. At one point, Cary Grant was sitting on one side of me, and Fred Astaire on the other. Thank goodness I didn't have to choose. I blushed. I giggled. I cheered inside. I introduced Tori and Randy to Cary Grant and Fred Astaire. Aaron laughed. He knew all about my fantasy men.

The party was a success. Fred and I didn't dance that night in the Chasen's tent, but we did at other times. His recording of "My Funny Valentine" is my all-time favorite song. Fred had earlier pointed out a man trying to slip one of the giant martini glasses into his wife's gift bag.

On his way out, Cary pointed to the wife of a famous Hollywood columnist who was dumping candy from the various candy dishes on the tables into her gift bag. "Happy Hollywood New Year," he laughed. (Today, I own a Fabergé cigarette case that Barbara Hutton gave to Cary Grant; I bought it at an auction.)

Life in Hollywood is like anywhere else. It's just more exaggerated.

I was afraid we wouldn't make it to 1989. Despite my love of horror and fantasy, a film I saw decades earlier, *1984*, frightened me so.

The 1956 movie taken from George Orwell's 1949 novel haunted and scared me for nearly three decades until the year 1984 finally arrived. When we were assigned the book in school, I refused to read it. The movie had been enough for me.

When I was a child going to movies, I didn't know words like *foreboding* and *totalitarian*, and I never really thought about differences between fact and fiction. I hoped there was no *House of Wax,* but it might have been kind of fun to visit (as long as I would be allowed to leave).

Orwell painted a picture of far-distant future 1984 that was as sad and depressing as I could imagine. People didn't look or act like the people I knew. Something was terribly wrong. Why did everything have a name, slogan, and a label? And why couldn't I get this "Big Brother" out of my mind?

Heads blowing off and melting corpses were nothing compared to the scenario in *1984*. As the decades passed, I waited with fear and dread, always thinking I should really enjoy life because Big Brother and his evil love-hating, freedom-fearing pals were going to take over.

The real-life 1984 was one of the best years for the Spelling family. Since Aaron's shows accounted for one third of ABC-TV's prime-time programming, the executives wanted to keep him happy. The four of us took a train journey across America (and back) to sail the QEII to Europe and enjoyed a family vacation far from the reaches of thought police or Big Brother.

I don't think of those fears very often today, unless I see or read a reference to the book or movie. I turn away. The movie might look silly today, the way my favorite TV series with 1950s spaceships and kitchens of the future look to us now.

But I'm not taking any chances.

I think I'll slip my copy of *Shall We Dance?* into the DVD player and escape for a little while. I still want to live a fantasy sometimes. Then I can go back to work.

Chapter 11

✖

There's a Lot of Funny Business in Showbiz

It seems as though there's nothing secret in show business any longer.

It's not just the tabloids that have the behind-the-scenes stories. The women's magazines, news broadcasts, Web sites, gossip columns, blogs, entertainment magazines, YouTube phone videographers, and water cooler and buzz gatherings all provide information about celebrities and what they're doing. It seems that everything's public.

Wrong.

I hate to tell you, but most of what you learn is what some marketing executives in a meeting want you to know as part of a campaign to sell you something.

Show business is a business, just like selling groceries or manufacturing lampshades. Not everyone is good at figuring out which movies will be hits, or what TV series will make it to syndication, but some people are really good at determining what the public should know in order to make them buy song downloads, movie tickets, celebrity clothing lines, or celebrity-branded tennis shoes.

As a people watcher, I find nothing more enjoyable than watching "showbiz people," including celebrities at various stages in their career, aspiring writers and directors making their networking moves, less-than-subtle agents and publicists pitching all the time, and the assorted characters who are expert name droppers and status seekers, and who think they're going to make it big with their next deal. You have to be fairly savvy to be able to make a living in showbiz over a long period of time, so those with longevity have to have special skills, if not big bank accounts. There's a lot of creativity and a great deal of talk about nothing—sometimes at the same time. When Aaron was at work I especially enjoyed the meetings at which people presented publicity strategies for how to make an actor appeal to a certain audience, or how to change an actor's image to attract ratings for a new show.

Since I started writing this book, I've been trying to figure out what I could reveal without being ostracized. To put it in perspective, I live in a place where the tabloid newspapers and TV shows run ads aimed at medical office receptionists, waiters, grocery baggers, and parking valets, offering them money for "confidential celebrity information" they might have overheard. Everyone is listening and taking photos. It can be quite profitable to be in the right place at the right time, but the odds of getting the "gotcha" are not that good.

When you live in a community where the most popular books have titles such as *Hello, He Lied; You'll Never Eat Lunch in This Town Again*; and *Indecent Exposure*, you get the idea that there are some strange rules and customs here.

Let me add some others.

One of my town's favorite activities is watching awards shows from private gatherings across town from the chaos, glitz, and glamour of the actual event. Why? First, there are only a small number of good seats at these awards shows, and these go to the most-nominated people and the present-ers. Everyone else is worried about his or her seat and how it defines them. Row MM? Yikes! It's better than the balcony, but too close to last year's loser. Seat 144 to the left? Not good, but better than those seats behind the pole. Sometimes it's safer to stay home, where there's no risk of being named to a worst-dressed list.

Besides, when you're not at the awards show, you can gossip and laugh—and tell the truth.

My favorite awards show activity is a guessing game. When I hear someone receiving an award talk about the "generosity" and "collaborative spirit" of the cast or crew, that usually translates to someone surrendering close-ups or lines to someone else during production (and chances are they didn't want them anyway).

One constant when watching awards shows is knowing that at least one—and probably more—of the winners is shaking as he or she leaves the stage not from excitement but from the fear that it's the end of his or her career. "I'll never top tonight," no one in particular will be told. "Who's going to hire me now that my price will go up? It's a terrible thing to happen at this point in my career." That's what you hear in between the stage and those fluffy backstage press conferences where the stars pull out the lists of names they said they forgot to thank earlier. Winners' angst is overwhelming.

Confidentiality agreements are quite common in entertainment companies and households. People have to promise that they won't talk about a script they think is bad, report that a star spilled his water, or that a dress didn't fit the not-so-petite starlet.

Even though I haven't signed one, I'm going to be discreet and tell some stories without naming names.

The dashing star of one of television's most famous series used to make frightening sounds—like birds in pain—each time before shooting began. When people would ask if he was hurt or ill, he'd explain, "I'm just trying to get my voice warmed up to make it deeper. My role and wardrobe demand a deep voice, and I can't disappoint my millions of fans."

An actor who played a debonair police detective really wanted to be a recording star. The first time I met him, he greeted me with "stereo or mono"? I didn't know what he meant. Aaron explained that he had just released a record, and wanted to know what equipment I had at home to listen to it with. Once he found out, he would sell people the album. Stereo, I discovered, cost a dollar more per album than monaural.

90210, the show that made one of Beverly Hills's zip codes the most famous in the country, was shot in the San Fernando Valley. Aaron rented a warehouse and turned it into a soundstage. He did the same for the series *Vega$*, but that one was actually in Las Vegas. *Melrose Place* was also miles away from the actual street, also in a nondescript Valley warehouse that Aaron transformed into hip and trendy Melrose Place.

One day a longtime wardrobe person on Aaron's shows called in sick. An office assistant went to a chic Beverly Hills store in her place to pick up pieces of wardrobe for one of the series. The salesperson told the young woman, "We'll just do the regular three-for-one arrangement, right?" Wrong. Fortunately, the assistant (who got a very big bonus) told us, and that's when we found out that our wardrobe person had been buying three of everything and charging Aaron. One outfit went to the production. One went to her closet. And the third was listed as a store credit in her name! We knew we were spending a lot on a genuinely expensive wardrobe, but we never dreamed the budget was three times what it should have been.

Some of the stars of our most elegant shows often deliberately threw off the shooting schedules so they could leave the lot wearing the show wardrobe. It was actually pretty transparent. It would happen on the final day of shooting, when no one was paying full attention to the clothes. Aaron knew it was taking place, but he let it go for a few years. "What was I supposed to say?" he would ask plaintively. "I'll get sued if I ask an actress to undress or unzip." This was often his lame excuse. I'd get so mad when I saw those famous and rich actresses on awards shows wearing those clothes. They belonged to Aaron!

Pilfering isn't uncommon; many people think they're entitled. A business manager once asked why our wallpaper budget was so high. What? "We have a five-figure wallpaper budget?" I asked when I'd seen the numbers. "Why do we buy so much wallpaper?"

I had insisted that the Carrington home and other glamorous locations on Aaron's shows have the same kind of wall coverings and furniture that a family with that amount of wealth would have. So the crew bought wallpaper, furniture, light fixtures, carpeting, and everything else that the rooms in exquisite mansions would have. I discovered that they also bought excessive quantities of spares, just in case.

We found out that people were sneaking rolls of wallpaper and carpeting off the set. It was hard to believe. These were well-paid people, and rolls of wallpaper and carpeting were big and heavy objects. But, alas, a Realtor I knew told me she was selling a home that the owners said had *Dynasty* rooms. Sure enough, the house belonged to someone we knew from the show, and his home had carpeting, wallpaper, and even some of the fake antiques from our show.

I recently had a meeting with some television executives, and we were trading stories about working with celebrities, discussing some of their, uh, unusual preferences and habits. One executive told me a funny story about a remote location shoot, and I told him about the *Dynasty* house filled with our stolen props.

"You'll never believe this," he said. "My wife and I have one of the actual tables from the Acapulco Lounge on *The Love Boat*." He explained that they had bought the house from the estate of a man whose name I immediately recognized as someone who had worked on several of Aaron's shows. "When we looked at the house and saw the table," the executive said, "we said it had to be part of the deal. The owner agreed, and it's in our bedroom. We love it. What a treat."

I like this man, and I'm glad he and his wife like the table, but my regard for our former employee evaporated. I tried to remember what he'd earned. It was a lot of money.

One of the scariest things was when people brought guns on a set. One *Mod Squad* co-star, who later admitted to a serious drinking problem, used to wave a loaded gun around between takes. A co-star of another series often ripped his pockets and got stains on his white jacket and pants because of his heavy gun.

Drugs? Yes. Enough said.

One early, edgy series of Aaron's featured three young stars who were to personify the coolest, hippest, trendiest, smartest, and most fashionable of the sixties generation. One of the stars asked Aaron to explain every line of dialogue, every gesture and every decision the character made. The star said it had to be "righteous." It was. The show ran for six years.

It wasn't all about being a babysitter, traffic cop, security guard, and ego-massager, but those were big parts of most Hollywood job descriptions.

Aaron got the most joy from casting the older stars on *The Love Boat*. He saw himself as a guardian of Hollywood's legacy and tradition, and realized there were very few jobs for these actors in young, hip, happening Hollywood.

The stars were grateful, most said they had a great time, and the shows created stories for all generations and nostalgia for some, and it introduced former stars to new ones.

"If my legacy is that I gave some of our most cherished stars a place to work, that's enough for me," Aaron used to say.

Turns out his legacy was bigger. Despite working with some of young Hollywood's biggest celebrities every year, it was his "oldies but goodies" he most valued. And as far as we know, none of them ever stole wallpaper or carpeting from the set.

Chapter 12

I'd Like a Thousand Shares of Pushkey, Please

I had just turned nine when I first heard the term *business manager*. As with a lot of my education about life, my teacher was Lucille Ball on *I Love Lucy*. The episode is called "The Business Manager," and in it, Lucy, as usual, has an angle on getting what she wants.

Ricky hires a business manager because the Ricardos are having trouble with the household budget. I remember Mr. Hickox was kind of a stern, crabby guy, and my father called him a "penny-pincher." That made me laugh. Why would anyone want to pinch a penny, and how many pennies would someone have to pinch to get rich, I wondered.

The business manager gives Lucy five dollars, which sounded like a lot to me. He told her that this would be her spending money for a month, which sounded reasonable, too. Movies were twenty-five cents then (Disney movies were thirty-five cents), a big package of gum was a nickel, soft drinks (when I was allowed one) were a dime, gumballs were a penny, and my other needs were basically covered. Lucy's were, too, I thought.

In true Lucy fashion, of course, she tries to figure out a way to make the money go farther. I thought her plan was really smart and thoughtful, too. She offers to buy groceries for her neighbors. She collects their money and then charges the groceries to a credit account the business manager has set up for her at the grocery store. She then has lots of cash, everyone gets their groceries, and it seems like a good arrangement. Lucy is sure happy, and Ricky seems proud that his wife is managing the budget so well.

That's when all the misunderstandings start happening. Ricky finds a wad of Lucy's cash, along with a neighbor's grocery order, "Buy Can All Pet."

Although by this point in their marriage, Ricky should have figured out what Lucy is doing—or at least tried to ask her, as she usually caves and confesses—he assumes she is successfully investing in the stock market and that the note is a stock tip.

While Lucy is buying a neighbor's pet food, Ricky buys "Canadian Allied Petroleum," despite the advice of the business manager.

Ricky makes a quick thousand-dollar profit, fires the business manager, and splits the cash with Lucy. "I suppose you're going to put it right back in the market," he says. He is right, for once. She does. She has charged just under five hundred dollars, and her money does go to the market.

I didn't understand all of it in 1954, but I thought business managers gave out money, credit was a good thing, and stocks turned a wad of bills into a thousand dollars and made husbands suddenly generous.

This all came back to me in 1968, right after Aaron and I were married. I wasn't devious like Lucy, and I didn't have trouble with the household accounts. I had actually been fairly good with money, but lived in fear of running out of it. My parents grew up during the Depression, and my grandparents shared horror stories of poverty with me. My father had his ups and downs in business, too. I first remember him losing his business when I was seven or eight, and after that, we never felt secure. Therefore, Lucy's schemes were too wild for me, especially when it came to risking money.

My allowance was bigger than Lucy's. Must have been inflation. Aaron gave me five hundred dollars a month from his paycheck to spend on "anything I wanted." We, too, had charge accounts for groceries, and I wasn't responsible for any household expenses. Plus, I actually had more money than Aaron did when we got married, having earned good money as a model and designer. Between my savings bonds, stocks, and checking account, I had over twenty thousand dollars, which was six thousand more than my new show business executive husband had.

I had wanted to invest earlier. My father had eclectic tastes in reading and in life. He taught me to read the *Daily Racing Form* and *The Wall Street Journal*. I didn't care much about horseracing until later, when Aaron started buying and racing horses, but I did like the subject of money, and I remembered Ricky's luck, when he didn't even know what he was doing.

When I was twelve, *The Wall Street Journal* ran some stories about Sears Roebuck & Co. I liked reading their catalog, and there was a store not too far away from our house. Long before I knew about press agents, I figured out that almost any publicity was good publicity. So I asked my father to invest a bond I had been left in Sears stock. He refused. When I was twenty-one, I did the math and realized that if my father had listened to me, I would have been a millionaire.

I was a good saver. I always put money away in what my mother called a "pushkey" account with "mad money." She told me I should always have money my husband didn't know about, "just in case."

So when Aaron gave me five hundred dollars to make sure I wouldn't have to go to him for money, I ended up saving most of it.

We had a business manager, who was nicer than I remember Ricky and Lucy's business manager being, but he didn't bother with my five-hundred-dollar allowance. I think he was just relieved that Aaron's new bride didn't ask for more. That was not the Hollywood norm.

Over the years I watched my pushkey account grow and remembered Sears and the imaginary Canadian petroleum company. It was time to invest. I didn't tell Aaron. I didn't tell our business manager. I just had fun.

I bought Disney. I remember thinking how smart they were to make all the good movies I had liked while growing up and then charge more to see them. I bought Coke because what else would anyone drink at the movies, and then added AT&T as I saw how routine and easy long-distance calls were to make. I made myself pink files, one for each stock. They were really pretty.

And I made more than a million dollars!

My stockbroker, a very nice and enthusiastic man, took the ride with me. We giggled as my stocks rose, and consoled each other when the prices went down. It was a very good time for the market.

In retrospect, my friendly stockbroker should have been asking questions, such as "Have you set aside any money for taxes?" "Is your husband proud of your investment expertise?" "Do you and Aaron have a business manager or accountant I should be talking to?"

Here's a warning. When you earn a million dollars and haven't paid taxes, eventually you have to do so. I decided to confide in our business manager. I sent him an envelope with information about some of "our" stocks. I figured I'd ease him into it, and then he'd tell me what to do, and then we could talk to Aaron, and . . .

Instead, the envelope ended up in Aaron's mail. I figured this out when he called me screaming. "You've got stock? Who in the world would buy Disney?" I told him this was a wonderful time to own Disney. He didn't seem to care.

Our business manager figured out the best investment strategy of all. He started a charitable foundation with the money I made in stocks, and this marked the beginning of a long and wonderful tradition of family giving to nonprofits.

There are so many ironies to this story. ABC Television, which would later be owned by Disney, was called Aaron Broadcasting Company for many years because Aaron provided so much programming to the network. Remember that *Mod Squad, The Love Boat, Fantasy Island, Charlie's Angels, Vega$, Dynasty, The Colbys*, and many of his other shows were all on ABC.

Lucille Ball was one of Aaron's first employers. As a young man, he moved to Hollywood because he loved the entertainment industry and wanted to see if he could make a go at a career. He began with small acting roles, appearing as "Gas Station Man" in the famous 1955 *I Love Lucy* episode "Tennessee Bound," with Tennessee Ernie Ford. Only after we were married and I saw a rerun of the episode did I realize that the skinny little guy with a Texas accent from my childhood *I Love Lucy* viewing days had become my husband a decade later.

In the 1980s, Lucy wanted to return to television, so she and Aaron teamed up on a show called *Life with Lucy* for (of course) ABC. Unfortunately, it did not work. Aaron took the blame, even though there was plenty to go around. I think the problem was that Lucy wanted to make *I Love Lucy*, but the audience didn't want to see her do pratfalls. During one taping, the script called for her to fall off a ladder, and when she did, the audience gasped. People were scared, and the scene did not play as a comedy. Lucy wanted the same writers and staff she had had decades earlier and was afraid to modernize her character. Aaron tried to make the show more modern, though he was very respectful of Lucy. Aaron was terribly disappointed in the show, and Lucy didn't attempt another television comeback.

In the meantime, I kept buying stock. I visited a Bed, Bath & Beyond store, the most amazing store I had ever seen. (Apologies to the stores on Rodeo Drive, which I've also said are amazing.) As a consumer, when I saw something wonderful and impressive that was well run, with a warmth and comfort like Bed Bath & Beyond, it was something I wanted to own. Over the years, with splits, dividends, and success, that stock has gone up more than 3,000 percent. More for charity through our foundation.

I also loved Corning products, and bought their stock. Unfortunately, I kept it too long, and lost most of my money. Later, I bought more stocks and made up for some of the losses.

I bought Garmin the first time someone showed me a GPS system. I knew everyone would need one of those. And they did.

I thought Blockbuster was a can't-lose. I lost.

I bought oil companies as gas prices climbed, and added to my Exxon and Chevron. Home Depot seemed like a good thing to own because it was always so crowded, and everyone was buying. Comcast, Bristol-Myers Squibb, and Merck all soon became part of my portfolio. Yes, by then it was a "portfolio."

I still have a pushkey account. And I have stocks my business manager doesn't know about (no names), and I have cash stashed for who knows what.

Mom taught me well, and I know why:

Here's an ad from the *Parents* magazine issue my mother was reading when I came home from the hospital:

MAKING YOUR WISHES COME TRUE . . .

One wish has been fulfilled. Won by 3½ years of deadly struggle. With God's help, we have prevailed.

Now we have a chance to make another wish come true. For most of us, the outlook is a bright one. If we simply use the brains, the will, the energy, the enterprise . . . the materials and resources . . . with which we won the war, we can't fail to win the peace and to make this the richest, happiest land the world has known.

Your wishes have been wrapped in that bright outlook. Your wish for a cottage by the lake. For your boy's college education. For a trip you long to take. For a "cushion" against emergencies and unforeseen needs.

You can make those wishes come true by buying bonds today . . . buying them regularly . . . and holding on to them in spite of all temptation.

There's no safer, surer investment in the world. You can count on getting back $4 for every $3 you put in E Bonds—as surely as you can count on being a day older tomorrow.

So why not be patriotic and smart at the same time?

Fulfill your wish—buy extra bonds in the great victory loan!

Thanks, Mom, for the advice. And, Dad, in retrospect, it's okay that you had me keep my bonds instead of buying Sears stock. They don't pay four dollars for every three-dollar investment these days, but they were steady, reliable, and enabled me to make more money later.

Chapter 13

❁

Sweets for My Sweet

My father always believed his son should study economics and his daughter should study *home* economics. It made sense to me. My mother was a superb cook, and my father enjoyed telling us that he paid for the food that turned into the great meals she cooked.

When I was eleven I wrote an article for our local newspaper to thank my father for the best gift ever. I called it "How I Gave My Father an Ulcer with My New Betty Crocker

Cooking Set," and I wrote about how I didn't know what I was doing and now I was being trusted to make actual food. I was seriously worried that my cooking experiments might not be good for my father—and then he developed an ulcer, whatever that was. I was sorry. He seemed amused, but he also seemed to enjoy my mother's cooking a little less. I soon graduated from my Betty Crocker set to the real thing, next to my mother in our kitchen, and we shared some of the best times ever.

My mother's kitchen was equipped with everything a 1950s cook would want, and we used every piece of equipment. She kept scrapbooks, folders, index cards, newspaper clippings, cents-off coupons with recipes on the back, handwritten notes from long-lost relatives, and magazine ads, totaling thousands of recipes, which I still treasure today.

"The way to a man's heart is through his stomach," my mother always said, quoting the unlikely pundit Fanny Fern, who wrote these words in 1853.

And our kitchen was the ultimate tool to satisfy the stomach and win the heart.

Our *Woman's Home Companion Household Book* suggested a new concept for kitchens in the late 1940s, and my mother was among the first to buy:

> . . . a desk and chair where you can plan meals, make grocery lists, and do all the other things which require thought and writing.

Sweets for My Sweet

This is very efficient and a business-like idea . . . and the addition of a telephone on the desk will, again, save endless steps.

She got the desk, chair, and phone, and many more of our future steps were confined to the kitchen.

Mom and I worked side by side, creating stews and stroganoffs, desserts and sauces, appetizers and seafood, entrees and hors d'oeuvres, everything from veal piccata to vinaigrette dressing, layered pear and Roquefort cheese salad, to no-bake brownies and bouillabaisse. When I look at her recipe books, I see her handwriting and mine, side by side, as we experimented together, sometimes improving the published recipes, sometimes further tweaking our improvised improvements. It was all there, from stuffed cabbage with sauerkraut to popovers, from soup to gingerbread cookies with extra whipped cream, tri-tip pot roast to sour cream coffee cake, from steamed lobster tails to fried chicken. Tori especially loved the chicken casserole, Cornish game hens, and sour cream coffee cake, and made sure she took those recipes with her when she moved out.

I excelled in cooking and sewing in school, which satisfied my own ambitions and those of my parents. I never aspired to higher office, but I became president of the Home Economics Club in high school. My father was so proud. And I won second place in the Gold Medal Cake Bake Contest. My mother announced I should have tried harder.

Cooking was so much fun. My cooking teacher let me cook for faculty meetings. Before that, it never occurred to me that teachers actually ate food, and now here they were eating my food! What a thrill.

Later, I became the cooking teacher's assistant and taught cooking to the freshman girls. I would start with the advice my mother always gave me: "Make sure all your ingredients are in front of you before you begin. There's nothing worse than getting well into cooking the meal and discovering you don't have everything." I remember the students in my class writing this down, and for about four seconds, I considered becoming a teacher.

I couldn't wait until Tori was old enough for us to start cooking together. When we had a chef, he or she would be exiled from the kitchen so Tori and I could bond the way my mother and I did. When Tori was little, I had the child-proof locks removed from two of the kitchen cabinets so she could delight in finding utensils and pots and pans that looked like mine. She especially loved banging her wooden spoon on the counter, and I remember wondering how my mother would have responded to such noise. I loved it. Maybe we'd open a restaurant together someday. But my plan didn't last long. Tori was too impatient, would decide we were missing ingredients, and then move on to something else.

My mother and I never stopped practicing. She was so organized (all right, so am I). We had a book full of bread recipes. Our favorite was monkey bread, and I remember her letting me write out the recipe, line by line, ingredient by ingredient, so we would always have it. She not only kept it, but made copies of it, which I found later in all of her notebooks and file boxes of recipes. Later, we modified it and made monkey bread popovers.

I loved baking the most, and my mother preferred cooking. We made a perfect team. I liked it when she gave me tips and we shared our cooking and baking secrets. She loved to pass along information she'd learned, assuming she agreed with it. She told me it was hard to fail at cooking. "If it doesn't come out right, you can always adapt the recipe," she said, as we adapted Betty Crocker, General Mills, Mr. Kraft, or whomever we were improving. That wasn't the case with baking, where the measurements had to be precise.

My mother was also good at *taking* tips.

She kept the dog-eared copy of *The Woman* magazine that she'd read during her pregnancy. She'd marked up the story "Are Drugstore Meals Good For You?," writing a big "NO!" on it.

The magazine answered its own question:

Yes, says this nation-wide survey of menus and preferences. The food sold at our soda fountains is well balanced, nutritious and economical.

"Don't believe this story," my mother told me. Of course, I would never have seen it had she not shown it to me.

Stating that twenty-five million meals were served in U.S. drugstores daily, the magazine reported, "Young stenographers and office workers are the chief patrons, and their grandmothers have been warning them: 'You'll ruin your digestion eating such food.'"

My mother was clearly on the side of the grandmothers. We never ate in a drugstore.

She and I also shared her favorite cookbooks, including *The Original Boston Cooking-School Cook Book*, the 1896 book by Fannie Farmer. Mrs. Farmer agreed with my mother about the importance of cooking. Her dedication thanked people for "promoting the work of scientific cookery, which means the elevation of the human race."

Neat. My mother and I were elevating the human race! Farmer continued:

Cookery is the art of preparing food for the nourishment of the body. Prehistoric man might have lived on uncooked foods, but there are no such races to-day who do not practice cookery in some way, however crude.

I wasn't so sure about that, but my mother assured me we were far away from anyone crude or prehistoric. I thought about Fannie Farmer whenever we visited one of the dinosaur exhibits at the museum. I knew they didn't practice the art of cookery, but it was clear they ate a lot.

I keep my mother's copy of *America's Cook Book* because I

remember how excited she was when she got it. She read to me that this fourth edition had "speed" and "ease" in mind. But the exciting part was that it had a whole section devoted to pressure cookers, and there were recipes from thirty-eight countries to "bring the world into your kitchen."

Becoming international was a great idea to me. I learned other languages with fancy-sounding words like *cordon bleu, soufflé, éclair, chop suey, goulash, spareribs Reykjavík, café brûlé, café diablo, kebab, chicken cacciatore, polenta con salsiccia,* and *egg foo yung.* Ooh la la!

One of the few times I was secure in life was when I was cooking. I loved cooking for Aaron when we got married, and there were many times when we didn't have chefs on staff. My specialty and his favorite was fried chicken, but he ate everything I cooked. He was most partial to anything fried that he could top with ketchup, but he also loved pork chops, my mushroom barley soup, chicken and rice (with my special onion soup), beef Bourguignon, and stew with lots of gravy.

The ultimate compliment came when my parents had a dinner party to celebrate their wedding anniversary, and they asked me to cook for it.

My biggest culinary mistake was probably the easiest job I ever had. One day Aaron said he wanted hot cereal, but I had never made (or eaten) it. I ran out and bought Cream of Wheat and couldn't wait until the next morning, when I would prepare it for him. Instead of looking like the picture on the box, though, it bubbled, formed lumps, and smelled really bad.

My willpower failed. I upchucked the smelly, lumpy, ugly stuff. I hit my stove and the counter, and ran around spreading my mess over the rest of my spotless kitchen. I was horrified. My husband was a remarkably good sport and so sweet.

"I'll just have toast, hon," he said. "I can make it." For the many years we were married, neither of us ever ate hot cereal or anything with lumps.

My kids were great eaters. Aaron usually worked late, so I fed the kids early. That part actually worked out quite well. I'd always present their food to them positively, as when teaching them to eat vegetables. Had I let them stay up late to eat dinner with their father when they were really young, they would have seen their father making faces and complaining about vegetables. This way, they didn't get any negative food messages. I wonder if that's in Dr. Spock's book.

When Randy and Tori moved into their first apartments, I gave each of them a copy of *The Joy of Cooking*. First, though, I added some of my handwritten notes on some of the recipes. My mother had taught me well, so I thought I'd pass along the cooking expertise to my own children. Later I learned that Tori had raided some of my recipe notebooks and file boxes containing mine and her grandmother's recipes. I should have been flattered, but I wanted my recipes back! (*Note to Tori:* Give them back.)

Sweets for My Sweet

Among the dozens of cookbooks in my kitchen are those my parents gave me as presents over the years. Each has its own words of wisdom.

My mother said she was constantly inspired by her *America's Cook Book*:

> Planning three meals a day for your family is a boring task only if you choose to regard it that way. Consider it a challenging game with high stakes and you and your family will both benefit. You'll find that they'll appreciate your efforts and you yourself will gain a real feeling of satisfaction.

By the time I started getting my own cookbooks, society was changing, and there were bigger challenges up ahead.

My 1960 copy of *Menus for Entertaining: 72 Parties and 400 Recipes for the Good Cook and Hostess* begins with:

> The civilized, three-star occasion dinner party has not completely vanished, fortunately. But the single standard of entertaining will not, we trust, return in any form.
>
> There are no formulas to rely on any more. You do have to stop and think.

I thought of my mother's little kitchen "business center," her place to stop and think and make grocery lists.

I liked three-star-occasion dinner parties, and I wanted to cook for one. I didn't worry too much, though. My book had formulas for summer (and winter), formal breakfasts for twelve, teenage parties for ten, Christmas Eve open houses for a hundred or more, and three chapters on the "Informal Summer Luncheon for 4." With all that learning to do, there wasn't much time to agonize about fewer parties.

One of my high-school graduation presents was *The New Good Housekeeping Cookbook*, an update of my mother's trusty old friend. This 1963 edition was talking right to me, as it identified groups of American women such as "young brides who valiantly cope with the complexities of new marriage" and "young high school or college graduates." I already knew most of the recipes, so I was way ahead of everyone else.

My new book had full-page color photos of hams, chicken curry, caramel apple dumplings, chocolate cinnamon tortes, and more. I thought that if I ever needed a change, some of these photos would be suitable for framing and would look good when I had my own kitchen walls to decorate.

When I did get my own apartment, my mother loaned me one of her true prizes, *The Cordon Bleu Cook Book*. It made me feel very important.

The Blue Ribbon, or Cordon Bleu, is of special significance to those who know and enjoy good food. . . . Originally, the term Cordon Bleu was used in France to designate noblemen who entertained their guests with supreme munificence.

I wasn't sure what that meant. I only knew that blue ribbons were tops, and my mother trusted me with her prized book. I memorized the glossary, which went from *artichauts* (globe artichokes) to *vin ordinaire* (table wine).

It's fun to look at the notebooks, makeshift recipe books, binders, file boxes, and sleeves for the clippings and coupons my mother and I shared over the years. Each has its own place in time, with my mother's early collections full of yellowing newspaper recipes from the fifties, sixties, and seventies, while my own newer books are more high-tech, with e-mail printouts and fax identifications across the top. The basic recipes haven't changed much, though.

I've played Mah-Jongg with a group of friends for many years, and they get such a laugh when I prepare a dish from one of those ancient recipe books or boxes. We're all always watching our weight, so we don't eat desserts every time we meet—just most of the time. Our current passion is anything "black cherry," although no one turns down butterscotch pudding. I also collect what I call my "junior cookbooks," with recipes packaged with titles such as *The Hollywood Bowl Cookbook* and *Taste of Texas*. I call on those recipes if one of my friends has gone to a recent Hollywood Bowl concert or has houseguests from Houston.

Living alone, I don't have much occasion to cook today,

but I love being in my kitchen, and will use any excuse to cook or bake. I get such a kick out of looking through our tattered *Easy Vue Recipe Book*, and laugh when I see that my mother tucked cleaning tips for removing food stains into the back of one of her file boxes.

My red notebook of recipes is the biggest and heaviest of the entire collection. It's the most contemporary, too, with everything from raw food menus—does that make me prehistoric?—to e-mail recipes for mandel bread. I have ads for cooking classes I'll never take, manuals for my kitchen convection ovens, and the original monkey bread recipe my mother copied and kept.

The majority of recipes are for desserts and breads, and I rate them—just in case I forget which evil treats I like the most.

Next to the recipe for Apple Puffed Pancake, I've written, "Great, 5/27/84." The Pumpkin Raisin Cake received my great rating on November 11, 1985. Old-fashioned Marble Cake won its accolades in 1978, the month Randy was born. Hmm. Even earlier, when Tori was two, I labeled Cocoa Apple Cake as "Excellent! 8/14/75."

Another Candy Spelling pattern?

At the back of my red notebook is a fax dated September 9, 1992. It's for a bland diet, designed to "ease symptoms of certain gastrointestinal disturbances."

I can't remember who needed this diet or why, but I do

remember my mother's cautions about eating drugstore food and digestive problems. I wonder if not eating at drugstores then allows me to eat cocoa apple cake now. If so, thanks for this, too, Mom!

Monkey Bread

Preheat oven to 400°F (according to Mrs. Marer), to 375°–385°F (revised by Candy in 1970s).

Ingredients

    2 cakes yeast

    ¼ cup warm water

    ½ cup sugar

    1 cup milk

    ½ cup butter (1 cube)

    1 teaspoon salt

    3 eggs, beaten

    3 to 4 cups flour

Soften yeast in warm water. Add sugar. Set aside.

Scald milk and put in big mixing bowl. Add butter, salt, and eggs. Cool to lukewarm. Add yeast mixture.

Add flour, beating well until soft dough is formed. Knead until smooth.

Allow to rise until doubled in bulk. Roll ¼-inch thick. Spread with melted butter, cut in diamonds, and arrange in greased ring mold. Let double in size. Bake 45 minutes, or until brown.

Courtesy of Gene and Candy Marer
Los Angeles, California
Circa 1956

Chapter 14

✻

My Mother's Gloves Were Off-White

My mother was a very elegant woman, but she didn't seem to know it. She would sweep into a room, and everyone would notice her. She had a regal presence about her. I always wanted to tell her what an impact she had with her grace and style, but I knew she wouldn't believe me.

And I didn't believe *her* when she told me that people noticed me. That was the last thing I wanted. I've always been painfully shy, and my aim was always to slip into a room unnoticed. I succeeded for a while. Marrying Aaron Spelling made it much more difficult to slip in anywhere unnoticed.

While my friends' mothers were like June Cleaver or Aunt Bea, my mother was like Auntie Mame—had Auntie Mame been a strict disciplinarian. She parented by fear, and I was always so afraid of making mistakes. She was elegant, ever ready for the next gala, dressed to the nines, and so wanted a perfect child modeled after her. I always felt like a failure.

My mother named me Carole Gene after Carole Lombard and my grandfather Eugene, but I heard those names only if someone was reading my name from an official government or school document or when my parents were angry with me. They started calling me Candy when I was just a few weeks old, my mother would tell people, "because she's so sweet." That's a nice image to maintain.

I like the name, but it's often difficult to be taken seriously when you're called Candy. Blond Candy. I'm just commenting, not complaining.

My mother's given name was Augusta, but everyone called her Gene, after her father. People said she looked like the beautiful actress Gene Tierney. She wouldn't say anything to this, except to remind them that she had named her daughter after another beauty, Carole Lombard.

My mother was also blond, but she dyed her hair red. I never knew why. She was so careful about her appearance, so beautifully dressed, so well coiffed. Her fingernails were long and red. She had beautiful clothing, and she made sure I was dressed in black and red taffeta, vests, layers of slips, delicate jewelry, shiny shoes, and all the beautiful things a pretty little girl should wear. She would talk about ways to look beautiful as she let me fill her evening bag with everything she needed for going out, starting with her lipstick, lipstick brush, comb, "ladies' room cash stash," and those non-filtered Chesterfield cigarettes that she made look unequivocally feminine.

I still have dozens of pairs of my mother's elegant gloves. I couldn't watch regal Audrey Hepburn in *Breakfast at Tiffany's* or trendsetting Jackie Kennedy on television and not think of my mother and her gloves. They were part of her class and grace, and a fashion accessory that has disappeared over the years. Too bad.

Those gloves weren't just a fashion statement. My mother was an expert at the "white glove test," always making sure everything was clean. No, not clean. Perfect.

Mirror, mirror on the wall.
I am my mother after all.

I enjoy admiring and touching my mother's tiny French and Swiss gloves, so delicate and intricate—and so small. She wore size six and a half. I marvel at the tiny buttons, hand-stitched detail, fine beadwork, leathers, hand-embroidered designs, and silks and cashmeres.

Looking back, I realize my mother didn't actually use her beautiful gloves to test for dust. She would take them off and use her finger. That explains why her gloves were ecru, off-white, and beige. They weren't designed for cleaning tests. They really were part of her elegance.

I'm not as good with my finger. I use gloves. Just below the drawers that now hold my mother's gloves, and my own designer gloves, I have some less-refined gloves that I use on mantels, counters, shelves, and anywhere else I think dust might have snuck in.

I'm a clean freak. My mother was, too, but she did it with more style.

I was brought up to be the perfect homemaker and house-keeper because that guaranteed that life would be wonderful. What man wouldn't love a wife who could keep a house spotless while wearing high heels?

My parents bought me little white gloves that looked like those that Mamie Eisenhower wore to church. Mine came with a little booklet that warned me not to smoke, drink, play cards, or put on makeup while wearing them. I didn't.

My treasured magazines told me that cleanliness was next to godliness in every facet of life. I never spotted a stain or mark when I saw photos of my movie star idols' homes.

One of my early issues of *Photoplay* magazine ran a big headline, "WHY HUSBANDS LOVE WIVES," and then, in smaller print, "To Shop at Stanley Hostess Parties." I couldn't wait to go to a hostess party.

I studied the ad, memorizing it. Stanley had dusters, mops, brooms, brushes, waxes, polishes, cleaning chemicals, and more. I had my heart set on the "extremely absorbent Amazo Mop," the Tan Swivel Mop ("to keep floors dustless"), and the E-Z Broom, "for easier sweeping." I had to have these. I started saving my money.

My childhood was in the exciting era of cleaner and whiter laundry, rolling portable dishwashers that were "gleaming porcelain inside and out," with a "flowing hot air blower for sparkly drying," and all kinds of new devices to minimize housework and make the home spotless. Even Salem cigarettes refreshed our taste, promising that the "air softens" with every puff. Wow, I could smoke Salem while doing laundry and, as Salem advertised in *Photoplay*, "Take a puff—It's springtime." My house would be fresh and clean and smell great from cigarette smoke, too.

My family made fun of me for my house-cleaning devotion, and my mother never thought it was very charming or endearing when I held up my little dust-dotted white glove and showed her why she needed to try harder.

If I had any doubts about the importance of keeping everything neat and clean, my first trip to Disneyland erased them.

I was only ten, but I'll never forget being greeted by bigger-than-adult-size Mickeys, Minnies, and Goofys, and they were all wearing white gloves! They must have been doing the white-glove test because all the trains, horses, monorails, steamboats, whirling saucers, race cars, submarines, and spaceships were spotless and antiseptic.

Beyond Mickey and Minnie, everywhere I looked were people wearing festive costumes and hats sweeping up trash. One happy worker told me that the streets of Disneyland were washed and steam-cleaned after closing each day. I now had a new goal in life, besides being the perfect wife: "I want to get a job here sweeping Disneyland when I'm old enough," I told my stunned parents.

By the time I was old enough to become a professional Disneyland sweeper, we lived an hour's drive away from the theme park. But I didn't have a car, and the concept of sweeping was a lot less attractive when I was eighteen. So I took jobs closer to home.

Besides, I had gotten married at seventeen, so it wouldn't have been too convenient. My husband was three years older, a senior when I was a freshman in high school, and we had dated on and off during my four years of high school. I liked him, and he had a cute convertible, but I think I liked the idea of getting away from the parents even more. We married right after I graduated from high school, and divorced after a couple of years. We never kept in touch, and our other high-school friends don't hear from him, either. In the meantime, I honed my housekeeping and cleaning skills in our small apartment.

When I married Aaron, at age twenty-three, I was on track to fulfill my aim and legacy to be the perfect white-gloved wife.

As my husband became more successful, we had bigger houses and more employees. We went from being in debt on a tiny house to having maids, butlers, chefs, and gardeners on the grounds of big houses. We entertained constantly. That's what successful moguls did, and I was Mrs. Successful Mogul.

We had lovely houses, wonderful collections, beautiful furniture, and I knew our parties would be just fine. But my shyness, combined with lifelong insecurities and the image of white gloves, convinced me that my house had to be perfect before anyone could enter it.

I would get up in the middle of the night, white gloves ready to be used, and "test" my house. I remembered those little spots I'd found at my parents' house, even though my mother and I were great housekeepers. I didn't want anyone finding any such spots at my house.

As far as I know, my reputation for having a spotless home is still intact. I've never lost my focus on keeping the ideal house. Even after my husband passed away in 2006, I've kept up a routine of being a tireless white-glove monitor. I confess that I do often perform the test on mantels, sculptures, counters, and tables, all hours of the day and night, weekdays and weekends, even holidays. I hope the security guards don't see me, but I suspect they do.

Only recently did I consider the possibility that I had passed a *90210*-like test.

When I was interviewing real estate agents to sell my

beloved home, The Manor (don't worry, my mother's gloves are moving with me), one of them, Brooke Knapp, sent me a note after she had visited my home. Here are some of my favorite excerpts:

A dream of everyone living in Los Angeles. And, what a privilege it was to drive into the motor court of The Manor. I felt honored, humbled and excited with anticipation at the same time. It is beautiful beyond my imagination. The style, the scale, the symmetry, the attention to detail . . . yes, the attention to every little detail.

The silver, not just in the silver drawers or the silver "closet" but throughout the house was polished beyond perfection . . . from the perfume bottle collection in the lower powder room to the cachepot holding an orchid on the landing of the second floor. The china was stored to perfection. The home is spotless . . . not just one day spotless . . . but days of spotless . . . years of spotless . . . with a fragrance clean and fresh . . . not of those candles people burn to cover other scents but real fresh.

What I came away from The Manor with was the extraordinary accomplishments of its Mistress and Designer/Builder/Guardian. In the end, I was humbled by her style, her creativity, her effectiveness at creating an oasis of great beauty, happiness, enthusiasm, love and excellence on every level . . . an accomplishment few even attempt yet succeed at.

There aren't many tougher critics than a Beverly Hills Realtor, who judges all the best houses.

I put the letter in with my mother's gloves. I knew they'd be proud.

Chapter 15

✻

Help Me, Oprah

There are six million hoarders in the United States, and I'm afraid I'm one of them.

I don't want to be a hoarder. I hope I'm not one. But I fear I might be.

My hoarding fear was heightened in 2007 when one of my friends e-mailed me a page from www.childrenofhoarders .com.

"Children of Hoarders," it read, "Oprah is looking for you."

It told the "children of compulsive hoarders" that Oprah Winfrey was looking for people willing to tell their family's "dirty little secret"—that they were "horrified, embarrassed and ashamed of the chaotic condition" of their parents' homes.

My heart stopped.

Oh no. When was Tori last on Oprah? How many times a year would they book her? Hadn't she been a guest recently, promoting a TV show or book in which she complained about me? They wouldn't let her on to add "living with a hoarder" to her list of childhood complaints, would they?

I thought about my son, Randy. No, the odds of Randy spending his time on a site called www.childrenofhoarders .com was quite unlikely. Besides, he liked to go on television only to talk about his own projects, not spill the beans about our family. (He has a successful life-coaching business. I wonder if he coaches people not to hoard.)

Okay. I was safe. My kids were not going to spill the beans to Oprah that they had a hoarder as a mother.

Once that immediate fear passed, I consoled myself with the realization that I'm a collector, not a hoarder. Yes, that's it. I collect things. I don't hoard them.

Since I knew Oprah would be doing a show on hoarding, I decided I'd better be prepared with answers just in case anyone I knew watched it. Deep down, I knew everyone would watch it, and think, "Oh, poor Candy. An Oprah two-part series, of all things. I hope Oprah doesn't mention her."

I headed for the study, where I keep every script of every

show my husband ever produced. I've never counted, but there are thousands of them, all bound in beautiful burgundy, beige, brown, yellow, royal blue, dark turquoise, British racing green, and white leather albums with the names and dates of the shows embossed in gold. Perfect. This was clearly a collection.

My *Merriam-Webster* dictionary usually helps me out: A *hoard* is "a collection of things kept for future use or need." Hey, hoarding doesn't sound that bad. And it certainly makes my husband's scripts a collection, not a hoard.

The dictionary helped further by defining *collect*: "to bring together into one body or place." Yes! My doll museum had all my beautiful dolls, accessories, sewing machines, and lots of other possessions in one place. Again, a collection, not a hoard.

My doll collection was originally Tori's. Over the years, I bought her beautiful dolls, and then our friends and family bought her dolls, and then, one day, she didn't like them. I never had dolls growing up; I preferred the company of stuffed animals, such as my substitute dog, Morgan. But I loved each of the dolls we bought for Tori, and thus began my collection . . . and then my doll museum, a light, airy, spacious room with a constant temperature of sixty-eight humidified degrees, special lights, stages, and a section for the anamatrons I bought for Aaron. It's a beautiful room, and people love to visit it. Nothing wrong there, Oprah.

Hoard as a verb means "to lay up a hoard of." (This is certainly not an expression I've ever used.) Its origin is Middle

English and comes from "to hide." These are ugly-sounding concepts. My collections are all beautiful, and need not be hidden!

And then I remembered my Beanie Babies. They were hidden away. What would Oprah say if she learned I had thousands—yes, thousands—of Beanie Babies stored neatly in special bags in closets? Would she shake her head if she found out I had paid collector's prices for some of them— does anyone remember when the Blue Elephant was going for five thousand dollars?—and that I made late-night trips to McDonald's for months every time a new mini Beanie Baby was offered? Would eBay's stock price drop if anyone realized that I probably accounted for a good part of its revenue by buying Beanie Babies online? Then I remembered that I had been motivated by thinking that Beanie Babies might be a good investment someday. Who knew the market would be flooded and the value would drop? If I keep holding on to them, though, I might make a profit.

I tried to find out if carefully packing things that could be worth something someday counted as hoarding. I couldn't find a reference. I decided I'd look at my Beanie Babies as savings bonds with no maturity dates.

My collection of Steuben glass is scattered (also neatly and, in some cases, artfully) throughout the house. My antique perfume bottles are out for all to see. I have a collection of antique crystal round or spherical ball clocks. (I dare you to find anyone who hoards those.)

My beautiful hand-painted fans are neatly arranged, and I look at them every day. That's a prized collection.

One day I was lost in thought trying to distinguish my twelve years of back issues of *Architectural Digest* (hoarding, I guess) from my hundreds of books about gardens (not sure which), when two intercom lines buzzed on two different phones.

I glanced over and saw six lines lit up. Uh-oh. Was Tori on television again talking about me? (I hoped it wasn't that seashell story. I really thought that was one of the nicest things a mom could have done for her little girl.) Had something happened to a friend? Had war been declared?

None of the above. Oprah's show on hoarding was about to begin, and the promo said it was going to be a two-parter.

For the next hour I sat fascinated as Oprah went "Inside a Hoarder's Home." I felt like taking notes, but I had years of notes on every possible subject that I never looked at. (Did that mean I hoarded notes, too?)

I joined millions of viewers (and apparently many people I knew) eavesdropping on Sharyn and Marvin, whom Oprah defined as having a three-thousand-square-foot house that "looks like a typical American home."

But, she went on: "Step inside, however, and the foyer has become a narrow passage walled by stockpiles of possessions. The kitchen is drowning in bags and boxes filled with unused items. The family room is unrecognizable, with every piece of furniture covered in heaps of miscellaneous belongings."

I couldn't wait for the first commercial break to do a quick inventory of my own house.

My foyer was as big and bright and uncluttered as ever.

The kitchen looked spic-and-span, although I knew there were stockpiles of paper towels and paper plates, and countless sets of glassware, dishes, china, silverware, pots, pans, salt and pepper shakers, and everything else. Not one bit of clutter, though.

Family room? Hmm, my house has a lot of rooms. I'm not sure which one is the family room, since the kids moved out years ago. I ran in and out of three rooms where we all used to like to congregate. All were recognizable, and I didn't find anything in heaps.

I got back to the TV in time to hear Oprah reinforce the idea that nearly six million Americans have a hoarding problem. I always say there's strength in numbers. I hate being alone.

She then announced that Sharyn and Marvin had seventy-five tons of trash in their home. "It would take fifteen huge Dumpsters to hold that much trash," Oprah said, and demonstrated by standing in front of a big blue Dumpster. "Imagine this amount of junk taking up every room, every hallway, every inch of space in your home."

She then described Sharyn and Marvin as "a husband and wife nearly buried alive in clutter."

I have 56,500 square feet of living space. If you add the attic and other storage, it comes to about 70,000 square feet.

I know what you're thinking. If 3,000 square feet could fill fifteen Dumpsters, how much could 70,000 square feet of hoarded items fill?

Now that Oprah had exposed hoarders—and even brought doctors in to help them—I decided I'd better make sure that I wasn't one.

I called some friends.

"Did you see *Oprah*? Do you think I'm a hoarder?"

I have nice friends. They said things such as, I'm a little eccentric, that the house is so large no one could hoard that much, and that I'm a collector. No one accused me of hoarding. I made a mental note to start stockpiling extra gifts to give them for the holidays.

I did get more careful about shopping lists. The next time we scheduled a trip to Costco, I decided we could halve the order of paper towels and toilet paper. I'm down to forty rolls of toilet paper and thirty-two rolls of paper towels. But half was still a lot.

I was also going to cut down on my order of dozens of bottles of window cleaner from the 99 Cents store, but I had read that the economy was hurting them. I didn't want to harm their business, so I still bought many more bottles than were necessary. We stored (not hoarded) them.

After Oprah's two-part show aired in November 2007, I became more conscious about how close I had come to being a card-carrying hoarder.

Knowing I would be moving to a smaller home someday

in the not-too-distant future, I made a deal with myself. For everything I brought into the house, I would get rid of twice as much.

I've just bought two T-shirts and donated seven to charity. (Surely, a true hoarder wouldn't give away *three* more than she promised, right?)

I checked out my stash from my home-shopping days on QVC and HSN and donated everything I had never opened. That cleared out a fraction of a shelf of one closet.

My first collection was Madame Alexander dolls, and I still have my first Pierre Poodle. I'm now struggling with what to do with them (and my doll museum) when I move to smaller quarters. I have a collection of video and arcade games. (Anyone for a game of Ms. Pac-Man?) The bowling shoes (every size, for men, women, and children) will definitely stay with the house's bowling alley.

Hoarders can't move to smaller places, can they? Yet that's my plan.

If I ever meet Oprah, I think I'll let her decide. She's nice. I'll show her jewelry, not Beanie Babies; crystal, not condiments; and my light and breezy foyer.

I'll take a picture of myself with Oprah and put it in one of my more than five hundred photo albums. No, scratch that. I don't think I'll mention my hundreds of books of photos to Oprah.

Candy Spelling's Collections

Alphonse Mucha advertising and beauty product posters

American and European Impressionist art

American and European Impressionist indoor and outdoor
  sculptures

American sterling peacocks

Antique Cartier clocks

Antique French golden bronze picture frames

Antique handkerchiefs

Automata

Bakelite jewelry

Ball clocks

Beanie Babies

Big Little Books

Blanc de Chine vases and objets d'art

Bronze match strikers

Bronze picture frames

Cabbage Patch Kids

Cachepots

China

Cookbooks

Couture books

Crystal

Cut crystal and antique candy dishes

Dinnerware

Dog paintings

Dresden butter pats

Erotic figurines

Etiquette books

Fabergé

Fine arts books on master jewelry designers

First-edition books (including Mark Twain)

Flower picture books

Gold presentation boxes

Herend hand-painted characters and figurines

Herend Rothschild Bird hand-painted china

Holiday decorations

Hors d'oeuvres plates

Lalique birds

Limoges boxes

Linens and doilies

Liquor decanters with silver overlays

Lorgnettes (opera glasses)

Mah-Jongg sets

Menu holders

Miniature fans

Miniature sewing machines

Music boxes

Perfume bottles with silver overlays

Photo albums

Place card holders

Porcelain and crystal butterflies

Royal Crown Derby figures

Silver and glass match strikers

Silver and porcelain swans

Silver birds and pheasants with movable wings

Silver salt cellars

Singing bird boxes

Snuff bottles

Sterling silver animals

Sterling silver band nodders

Steuben animals and collectibles

Sugar sifters

Table boxes (sewing, cigarette)

Themed salt-and-pepper shakers

Turtle soup dishes and matching spoons

Vienna bronze animals

Chapter 16

✤

Up, Up, and Put Away

When I first heard the Fifth Dimension singing Jimmy Webb's "Up, Up, and Away" in 1967, I was in love with a man who refused to fly.

But I knew I could change him.

After all, I loved to travel and to fly, and I planned for us to travel all over the world and share once-in-a-lifetime experiences with each other.

Aaron Spelling traced his fear of flying to his service in the

Air Force during World War II. He was yanked from a flight two minutes before it took off because he was sick with the flu. That flight crashed, and everyone on board was killed. Since he was expected to be on the plane, the military notified his family that he had been killed. When he arrived home later that day, his mother saw him and fainted—and when she regained consciousness, she made him promise never to fly again.

But he was going to marry the girl who grew up watching (and falling in love with) the handsome character who was introduced with the words:

Look! Up in the sky!
It's a bird.
It's a plane.
It's Superman!

I was dreaming of my Superman with whom I could soar to new heights of ecstasy.

A few months before Aaron and I got married, the Drifters hit the music charts with more high-flying lyrics in "Up on the Roof."

Everything pointed to upward. Man was about to go to the moon. Aaron and I would ascend to new heights together, too.

But he never did break his promise to his mother. We

never flew anywhere together. We had some spectacular vacations, by car, train, and boat. And I'm not complaining.

It's just that something had gone wrong with my scenario.

The highest we ever went together was our attic, and that's far from romantic.

My attic was a well-kept family secret and a source of much laughter and eye-rolling between Aaron and me. Now that I have put my home on the market and am getting ready to move, I do have to go up, up, and away, and figure out what to do with everything that's up there.

I hadn't given it a lot of thought until one of the Realtors spotted a stairway going up from the second floor and wanted to know where it led.

"To the attic," I mumbled.

"How big is the attic?" the Realtor asked—innocently, I'm sure. "Mumble, mumble, oh, about seventeen thousand, um, square feet."

"Huh?"

And then we went up to the attic.

He was speechless. I thought it might be a little overwhelming to a first-timer. I go up there so often that it's just routine for me.

Now it has become a math problem, and math's not my favorite subject.

I have an attic that covers just over 17,000 square feet. I'm moving into a new condominium that will be a total of

17,000 square feet. My current living space is 56,500 square feet.

The arithmetic goes something like this: 17,000 − (56,500 + 17,000) = much less space—and my having to get rid of an awful lot of possessions.

My attic is a source of amazement to the few people who had previously seen it. Much of what operates the house, from the heating and air-conditioning units to the mechanical lift that raises and lowers the chandelier in the entry hall, is housed in the attic. (I'm told that the lift was over-engineered so that it could raise and lower something as heavy as a Volkswagen, but I can't imagine why I'd want to hang a VW in my entry hall.)

The attic, like the house, is shaped like a *W*. Originally, the house was going to be called L'Oiseau ("Bird") but my French pronunciation isn't that good, and we liked "The Manor" more. I never considered the name Tara, although I have a staircase that Scarlett O'Hara would have descended beautifully.

My doll-designing rooms are in the attic, and I store many dolls there that are not on display in my downstairs doll museum. I've got the fabrics from which I made their clothes, and the drawings, color swatches, paper samples for boxes, and everything else an efficient doll designer would need. There are probably some non-necessities, too, but once I'd found stands to hold doll wigs and doll-size hair blowers, how could I resist?

We also store lots of extra household supplies. There are lightbulbs—more than sixty-five varieties. (I don't know how many light fixtures there are in The Manor, and I'm not going to count.) I know that sounds like a lot, but we have to keep them somewhere, and I never know when a dome light on the driveway, a reflector in the koi pool, or a custom light over a Renoir might need to be replaced. A quick trip to the attic handles all lighting needs.

I keep batteries adjacent to the lightbulbs. I guess there are hundreds of them, too, in all sizes and shapes and volts and expiration years. Name a volt, and we have it. The new owner of my house might laugh when he or she sees the battery and lightbulb collections, but I can guarantee they'll thank me later. That doesn't even include the rows of light panels that control the lighting throughout the house.

Do you know how much space it takes to store yards of extra carpet in a house such as mine? Think about that if you're criticizing the size of my attic. There are carpet pads, too. Any idea of how many air-conditioning filters this house needs? I don't know, either, but there are stacks and stacks of them.

There are fifty-nine boxes of Easter decorations. I have Easter eggs in different sizes and shapes from all the years different charity groups brought kids to The Manor for Easter egg hunts. I also have the bunny costumes (Easter, not Playboy) my kids wore to parties. Box 48 reads, 1 GIANT EASTER BUNNY. There are three boxes of new VARIOUS FOILED

EGGS and three more labeled PAINTED WOODEN RABBITS. Oops, I forgot about the pink grass, yellow grass, and green grass I bought for next year's Easter baskets and those boxes of new baskets. Oh, look, box 59 has 2 RABBITS AT A TEA PARTY.

I love holidays.

My boxes of Thanksgiving decorations include garlands for the various fireplaces in the house and Thanksgiving bears.

Halloween is one of my favorite holidays. My supplies include sound-activated jack-o'-lanterns, witches with caldrons, life-size (but not lifelike) ghosts and skeletons, beautifully carved artificial pumpkins, and even an animated spirit ball with a homely old lady who yells out threats to passersby.

There are ~~128 143 151 164 168~~ 180 boxes of Christmas decorations.

I love Christmas. For years I've been collecting toy soldiers (130 at last count, including 4 seven-footers), wreaths, dogs in Santa suits, tree ornaments, festive dishes and glasses, Mrs. Claus dresses for dolls, cones, tree stands, lights, sheet music, fake snowflakes, elves, and sleighs. There are bears who sit on my front steps every Christmas, those who sit on the entry stairs, and bears who sit on coffee tables. I have pastry chef bears who adorn the kitchen during the holidays, and one who has a little cast on his front leg. (I imagine he went skiing during the holidays, so I keep him in my office, where I can keep an eye on him. I count on him to keep an eye out to make sure the garland for the left side of the staircase doesn't end up on the right side. He has a good eye.) You name it, and I have it.

Anyone having a birthday party? I have dozens of boxes of streamers, candles, tablecloths, hats, cake platters, cake recipes, and more. I love birthdays.

I also love babies. That's why I still have the beautiful Royal prams Barbara Stanwyck gave Tori and Randy when they were babies. I can't walk by them without smiling.

I've quoted a lot of books in this book. Oh, boy, do I have books and magazines and videotapes and DVDs! There are hundreds of boxes of those in the attic. (I don't have to esti-mate how many there are in the rest of the house, do I?)

I love my books. There's everything from Dick and Jane primers to a college physics textbook that a houseguest left behind, from directories of Hollywood unions to home deco-rating books, from caring for orchids to child care.

My *Photoplay* magazines are kept in order, in plastic, proudly on display on special shelves. They are Hollywood history. They deserve a place high above all else, up, up, and away.

The attic houses various sizes of tapes and DVDs of every television show and movie my husband ever made, plus ex-tra scripts, notes, photos, memorabilia (anyone for a *90210* lunchbox or a *Vega$* poker chip, a *Charmed* book bag or a cast portrait of *Charlie's Angels*?). In order to explain why I have shelves and cabinets full of carefully organized boxes representing my husband's work, let me recap that he produced more television than anyone in history. In 1983, the *Guinness Book of World Records* saluted Aaron by naming him the "most prolific" television producer in history because of his astounding 3,842 hours of television shows. Guinness determined that someone could watch prime time seven nights a week for three and a half years without ever seeing a rerun of an Aaron Spelling show. That was in 1983. Now it's more than 4,500 hours of programs. That's why I have hundreds of boxes in the attic, plus rooms full of his awards, honors, favorite photos, original scripts, and shows throughout the house. I love my husband's work.

There's a hair salon in the attic. Why is it in the attic? We forgot to make room for it in the house. I like it. It's near one of the stairways and has a barber pole outside that used to make my husband laugh. The place is decorated like an old-style salon, with pictures of all the hairstyles from the fifties and sixties that, for some reason, we all thought were flattering and fun.

Oh, and there's a gift-wrapping room.

I know, I know. I wrote about how my gift-wrapping room is adjacent to my office on the first floor.

Well, there's a second gift-wrapping room in the attic.

And, then, hiding in the attic is the really large gift-wrapping area, for the really large packages.

While my downstairs gift-wrapping room is festive, my attic gift-wrapping room is all business, with big boxes, industrial-strength wrapping paper, heavy-duty tape, wire cutters, postage scales, reams of paper with eight-hundred-foot rolls, a shrinkwrap machine, straw, and anything a UPS store would ever need. I have a little kitchen next to it, since once I start wrapping those big packages, I sometimes won't emerge for hours.

By the way, everything in the attic is neatly labeled, cataloged, and stored.

HAND-PAINTED CACHEPOTS FOR ORCHIDS, CARD TABLES, FABRICS FOR BEACH HOUSE, PARTY FAVORS, REFRIGERATOR SHELVES, DRAWER PULLS, STUFFED ANIMALS, MAH-JONGG SUPPLIES, HARDWARE HINGES, TORI'S SWEET 16 SEAT CUSHIONS, MONOGRAMMED HANGERS, and ROOFING MATERIALS are some of the categories. Seriously.

If you want a sky blue Easter egg, I can point you right at it. Need a wreath that measures 16.6 inches? Miniature flowers? Custom glass for the lampposts at the bottom of the driveway? Plans for every inch of the house in ⅛-, ¼-, and ½-inch scale? It's all there.

Wait. I haven't accounted for all 17,000 square feet yet.

I also have a luggage section. I love luggage. There's every size, lots of different designers, various colors, and they all have special names. I remember while I was growing up my father had the "two-suiter" and "clothing bag." It's much more fun today. I've got too much luggage, I'll admit. I always pack too much. And I still have more, in case I ever need eighty or ninety suitcases for a family vacation. As I said earlier, we borrowed suitcases from the set of *Hotel* earlier in our marriage when we traveled. I guess we went overboard after that series went off the air.

I'm very sentimental about everything in Tori and Randy's life. I guess that explains why I've kept almost everything of theirs.

Do you want to see what Randy wore for Halloween in 1982? Got it.

The beautiful mother-daughter taffeta dresses Tori and I wore? Got them, too.

The custom seat covers I had made for Tori's Sweet Sixteen party so the girls wouldn't have to sit on the hard rental chairs? Yup. Right near the luggage.

I can walk through the attic and remember the happy memories just by looking at the boxes. Yes, they're numbered and labeled, too, with a Polaroid picture of whatever's inside attached to every box. It's easier that way, in case Randy wants to see what he wore on his first day of kindergarten. He looked so cute in his little school uniform, with gray pants, a navy blazer, and a red tie. (Aw, come on, Randy, don't you want to see that outfit? Tori, do you remember all those beautiful frilly dresses by Florence Eisenman? I don't know if I can keep them when I move.)

I have quantities of spare gifts like you wouldn't believe. There are very high expectations for a "Spelling gift," and I always used to take the advice of the Boy Scouts to "be prepared."

Up, Up, and Put Away

I love to give one-of-a-kind gifts. There's a wonderful store in Los Angeles that makes handmade personalized candles designed to be burned once a year for the first twenty-one years of a boy or girl's life. I received them for my children, and love to give them to other people for their blessings. My favorite gifts are those pertaining to something the recipient is interested in. That can be a book about a favorite subject, or a part of an antique collection. I like to surprise people with unexpected and unusual gifts.

If a colleague of Aaron's liked eighteenth-century paintings, he was confident he could call and I had one waiting to be wrapped and messengered. How about an antique clock? Got 'em. A duplicate Lalique piece that I didn't need for my own collection? Sure. Fountain pens when people gave them for graduation presents? What color?

There's also a kitchen equipment section. Aaron and I had various chefs at different stages of our life. When we entertained a lot, we had a chef who liked to cook for big groups. If we decided to eat healthy foods only (which we did rarely), we'd hire a macrobiotic cook. There's an expert for everything in L.A., and cooks who specialize.

The result was a lot of turnover in kitchen appliances, tools, pots, pans, bowls, and everything else a chef uses. So, when a new chef would come in with his or her list of necessities for my kitchen, we would move the last group of expensive former necessities to the attic. I always hoped that one chef would like what we'd bought for the last one.

Nope. Who knew there were so many different kinds of waffle irons and spice racks?

I'm trying to be mature as I tell myself, and anyone who'll listen, that it's time to downsize. I know people make fun of me for saying I'm downsizing to 17,000 square feet. That's a very large home, and I'm grateful to be able to have it.

Even if I just give away everything in the attic, I'll still have more than three times as much stuff as my new home will hold.

I don't think self-storage is the answer. Actually, one of those companies might want to talk to the new owner of The Manor about leasing space.

Yes, I'm going to be mature and businesslike and figure out how to downsize. I have to be less like a sentimental wife, mother, and grandmother and more like a corporate efficiency expert. It might work. I have hardhats, clipboards, and tape measures stored in the attic, too, so I won't have to buy anything new to take on that new job.

That's the math.

Chapter 17

❦

And Now a Word from . . .
Everyone Else

S o, now, the end (of the book) is near, and my insecurities
are running rampant. I had no shortage of them to begin with,
and now I realize that "Candy Spelling" is going to be listed
next to "Aaron Spelling" in some libraries and bookstores.

What was I thinking? Aaron's stories could be traced to
growing up poor in Texas, with the movies being his escape
from the realities of the times. He loved stories, paid special
attention to the plots, and imagined himself in the tales,

interacting with the other characters and even changing the directions of the plot.

Aaron was truly a Walter Mitty–like character, with a delightful imagination and his head often in the clouds. He loved fantasy, and loved making up fantasies in which he could live. He and television were made for each other, and he enhanced the entertainment experience for everyone.

So, I committed myself to competing with Aaron?

I had a lot of fun writing this book. I've learned new technology and about speech-recognition software, am struggling to figure out when to use quotation marks or italics, and if question marks go inside or outside and when. I've developed new anxieties agonizing over almost every word and wondering if I've done the right thing by writing this book at all.

Politicians send up trial balloons. I went to my friends. "What am I doing? Can I write a book? What have I done?"

Much of the anxiety (as if I needed more) came from the people closest to me.

"Candy, you're not going to write about [embarrassing story 4,895], are you?"

"Candy, be sure you put in the story about when we . . ."

"Candy, do you remember when you and Aaron . . . ?"

"So, Candy, I hope you're going to get back at Tori for saying those terrible things about you."

All right. I'm good at following instructions. My mother and Aaron taught me well. I want to please everyone. I want to thank everyone.

And Now a Word from . . . Everyone Else

I decided to officially ask people what they thought should and should not be in my book. Here's one piece of advice:

First, to my friend Denise Simmons, I'd love to tell the story about that afternoon in Century City with the kids, but my lawyer says it might have been a misdemeanor. Even though the statute of limitations is up, I can't tell.

Yes, I will admit to the time in New York when I said I'd get a cab and ended up hailing a limo. I'm from California. There were seven of us. It was freezing cold. I've seen this in the movies. I took out a wad of cash, stepped into the street, and the limo stopped. I would have hiked up my skirt, like Claudette Colbert did in *It Happened One Night*, if that's what it took. I sat up front with the driver. What's wrong with that? It was cold, and we got back to the hotel fast, didn't we?

❆

I asked my son, Randy, how much he remembered about our 1984 vacation in Europe, since he was only five. He remembered some of it, and of course we documented every moment in pictures, but he said he would never forget the trip he and I took in 2006. He's a writer. I'll let him tell the story:

When we were packing up to go somewhere else, I would have to help you pack due to the enormous volume of clothes . . . I mean ENORMOUS. You just kept bringing them out of the closet, and I thought, this is CRAZY! Not to mention, everything had to be un- packed when you got there.

Then, everything had to be packed exactly how it was. This means tissue paper folded around and in between everything!

I would have thought you had a side business in Italy and Paris wrapping gifts with the amount of tissue paper you had.

Then I would have to sit on the tops of the suitcases to make sure they closed. The most disturbing part was everything we would pack would be so meticulously placed in the suitcases, the thought would hit me that all this has to be unpacked just to be repacked up again. It was a vicious cycle.

One morning, in Venice, I woke up and called Randy's room. He wasn't there, and I got worried. When he returned, I told him how scared I was.

"I couldn't sleep, Mom," he told me. "I had a nightmare about packing your clothes in another hotel room, and had to go out for a walk around the city to clear my head."

❀

My lawyer, Stephen Goldberg, thinks Aaron and I should have been a comedy team. He wasn't sure if I should tell the story, but hey, Steve, you brought it up, so here goes:

In early 1993 Aaron and I went to Las Vegas. A friend told us that the Dunes Hotel was closing in a few days, but they were letting in a few guests, and it might be a nice private place for us to get away.

It was. They gave us the entire sixteenth floor, and the seventeenth-floor pool and gym were ours, too.

We looked forward to spending some time off together and took our six-month-old bichon frise, Shelley, with us. Aaron reminded me that Shelley wasn't quite housebroken, but I assured him it wouldn't be a problem. We'd always had wooden flats made for our dogs that we would place outside the house, and doggie doors so they could get out to "go" anytime. We'd put grass on top of the wooden flats, and we and the dogs were happy.

I shipped a flat ahead of us with our luggage, and the hotel arranged for lawn and seed to be put in the flat before we arrived. All set, I told Aaron. His only responsibility would be to take Shelley to the seventeenth floor, where we had the flat, so she could do her business.

The first night, my husband, the most successful executive in television history, was awakened by the puppy, and the message was clear. "I have to go." While putting on a robe over his pajamas, Aaron said he was worried someone would see him with Shelley. "No," I assured him. "We're alone on the floor, and no one will be at the private pool at four A.M." "No one but me," he replied, as he headed out.

My husband was not happy when he returned. "She won't go. It was freezing up there on the pool lobby, and the dog wouldn't go."

I asked him if he'd told Shelley to go on the flat.

He assured me he had.

"Go back, Aaron. The dog has to go."

Aaron was a nice man. He and Shelley headed upstairs again.

They returned. It looked to me as though the dog's eyes were watering. Aaron's eyes were red. He told me something must be wrong with the dog because she just wouldn't go.

I called my vet at home in L.A. and woke him up. Looking back, I have to give him credit for being so polite.

"Candy, she won't go on the flat because there are no smells. She doesn't know she's supposed to use the flat or that the lawn is hers. Someone has to pee there first, so she can pick up the scent."

I told Aaron this.

He refused.

"Aaron, look at her. She's going to burst."

"Candy . . ."

The standoff finally ended as it was getting light outside. Aaron and Shelley disappeared.

When they returned, the dog looked happier.

"Did you do it?" I asked my husband.

He refused to answer except to say, "The dog went."

To this day, I still don't know what happened. And I just can't visualize my prim and proper husband peeing on a flat of grass on a hotel pool deck. I don't think he went into the bathroom or left the suite with any kind of container.

I wouldn't be surprised if he found someone and paid him to pee on the flat. I didn't ask. But Shelley went from then on.

"Candy, can we leave the dog home next time we travel?" Aaron asked. "This was not the relaxing, romantic start to our getaway you promised me."

"Of course," I assured him. "Let's go back to bed."

Shelley jumped into the bed with us. She spotted the mirror over the bed, now that it was daylight, and she apparently determined the reflection was another dog in the bed with us. She barked for an hour. Aaron didn't speak to me the rest of the day.

I wonder if Aaron told anyone how he got the scent on the flat, or if this will remain one of life's mysteries.

⌘

My friend Willy Ehrlict, whose husband was also a successful television executive, said, yes, I had to tell my stories. She says she gets scared every time she hears the words *Candy* and *vacation*. The first story was when we decided to go to Palm Springs, and even though I rarely drove, I decided to drive. Willy looked like she was going to hide under the dashboard, and claimed I was going a hundred miles per hour on the freeway.

With all due respect to Willy, we were going faster—110 miles per hour—and I had two good reasons for driving so fast. When I had had my car serviced, the mechanic said I should drive it really fast once in a while because of its big engine. And I needed the driving practice.

I didn't realize we were going 110 until I glanced at the speedometer. I was gripped by fear, so I think I pushed down even harder on the accelerator. I just remember Willy turning the color of the white dividing lines on the freeway. We were in the fast lane, and suddenly, I was afraid I would hit the middle barrier. I swerved to change lanes. It felt instead as if we'd changed states, as the car was really flying! I felt like a teenager again, driving along to one of those Beach Boys songs about Daddy taking the car away if I got caught.

Aaron made me get rid of the Corvette I had when we got married. One time, when we were driving to his house, I went so fast around a curve that the car did a wheelie. "That's it," he declared. And my Corvette was history. I was relegated to my mother's used sedan, which lacked the glamour and speed I wanted.

Willy drove home from that weekend trip. I didn't look at the speedometer, and she seemed calm. Now that I think about it, I don't think she's been in my car since.

❀

Willy thought I should tell another travel story. She ended her e-mail with, "The more I think of it, I am pretty lucky to have survived our friendship SO FAR. First you lock me out of my room in the middle of the night and then you take me on a joy ride at 100 mph."

As Willy knows, I didn't deliberately lock her out of the two-bedroom suite we were sharing in Las Vegas. (We flew, not drove, by the way.)

Willy and I went to Las Vegas for a jewelry trade show. During the day we'd go our separate ways, then catch up in the suite's living room at night. I liked to stay up late and gamble, and she liked getting a full night's sleep.

One night, I was ready to go to bed early, so I took a sleeping pill. Willy was already in her room. After a while, when I still couldn't sleep, I decided to go downstairs to the twenty-four-hour, all-sweets-and-junk-food-and-magazines-all-the-time store to get some goodies. I knocked on Willy's door and said, "I just took a sleeping pill, so if I'm not back in fifteen minutes, come down to the lobby and look for me."

I was awake enough to buy a large Hershey bar, cheese puffs, Junior Mints, and assorted packages of cheese and crackers. I returned to our suite, double-locked the door, sat down at the bar, and proceeded to eat my treats.

I thought I heard someone knocking at the door a few minutes later, and thought how rude it was for someone to knock in the middle of the night. I kept eating. About ten minutes later, the phone rang.

"Candy, let me in," Willy said.

"Where are you?"

"I went downstairs to look for you. I looked everywhere and finally came back upstairs, and I was locked out."

I let her in. We both ate sweets. My sleeping pill never did kick in.

✄

On that same trip, I won a lot of money on a slot machine. My friends say that I have a kind of special "communication skill" with the machines. I don't. There *is* some rubbing of the machines involved, but we won't go into that. That night I sat at the machines for many hours raking in the wins. The casino was so happy with the amount of time I was playing the slot machines that they delivered ice-cream sundaes right up to my machine just to keep me there.

I remember the night well. I was using my "money management" method, starting with a five-dollar slot machine, then a ten-dollar, then twenty-five, all the way to the hundred-dollar slots. My method is to play with the casino's money. Every time I win, I take back part of my winnings, so I'm always playing on their money. (That is, when I'm winning.)

I'd worked my way up to the "top dollar" machine, which had a little picture on the left side that advised the player whether to take an offer. I ignored their recommendation. I knew they weren't on the player's side. And, lo and behold, I hit the big jackpot.

Willy was already back in the suite, so I called her and said I needed to show her something. When she saw the machine, she screamed so loud that people came from throughout the casino to see why she was screaming. I was sitting there in shock. There was so much hoopla and celebrating, and I remember saying I'd take my winnings in cash. I wasn't thinking clearly.

The casino officials started piling up the money. It didn't stop. Bills were everywhere.

Willy and I gathered up all the piles of money, asked a security guard to get in the elevator with us, and went back to our room. We threw the money on the bed. I felt like we were in one of those bank robbery movies and the feds were going to break down the door at any minute. We didn't have suitcases full of money or rubber bands to separate the bills, like in the movies. We just had tons of cash.

Willy and I counted it and made neat piles. Counting my other winnings, it came to more than $100,000. There was something reassuring and comforting about all that cash. In retrospect, when I think about it, I realize how dangerous it was. Wait. It gets worse. We stuffed the money into our baggage, purses, and paper bags and flew home with it.

I wouldn't blame Willy if she never flew with me again, either.

❦

A lot of the stories my friends told me to tell or keep secret have to do with food. Randy nailed one of my little habits:

In high school, I would love coming home with my friends because a lot of the time my mom would be in the kitchen baking something or making sandwiches. My favorite mom sandwich is sourdough bread, mayonnaise (she puts lots), tomato, avocado, sliced chicken or turkey and sprouts.

Of course, it was evenly spread to cover all of the bread (a habit I inherited myself) and salt-and-peppering everything evenly.

Randy now understands why sandwiches need to be even. Isn't it irritating to be eating a sandwich and run out of either bread or meat? The middle can't be thicker than everything else, or the last bite won't be as good as the first. Who wants to end up with a chunk of meat?

I have been caught taking apart sandwiches in restaurants to make them even. One time I was busted at the famous Nate 'n Al's deli in Beverly Hills. The owner came over to our table and asked if there was something wrong with our sandwiches.

"They're not even. There's too much meat."

He later told me I was the only customer who had ever complained that the sandwich had too much meat.

My friend and decorator Bob Dally has a food story about a trip we took to Paris to buy furniture for The Manor. "It might be kind of funny to tell the chicken-in-the-bag story when you and Carole Haber had me thinking that chicken was cooked in a paper bag," he e-mailed.

During that trip we went to a restaurant where no English

was spoken, except by Bob, Carole, and me. Carole was a French teacher, so we weren't worried.

"Here's chicken cooked in a bag for two," Carole said, looking at the menu. Bob and I decided to split it.

A huge chicken arrived, and it looked to me like the bag had veins running through it. Bob laughed and said that was silly. It had only been cooked in a bag. The "bag" was like a thin, fine balloon, very delicate, with the chicken inside. Something wasn't right. Those were veins, I kept saying. I was right. The "bag" turned out to be a pig's bladder, and our chicken was inside it. It took Bob years to get over it.

※

My friend Alicia Rose reminded me about a number of rushed dinners she and I had had. For most of our marriage, Aaron worked very late. I would feed Tori and Randy early and then wait for him. Most nights we stayed home and had a quiet dinner together.

When he retired, he'd encourage me to go out with friends; he was content to stay home, as always.

Alicia and I started going out to dinner, and the pattern was always the same: Aaron would call every five minutes. "Are you there yet?" Five minutes later, he'd call. "Have you ordered?" The next call would be to ask if our food had arrived. Then if we were having dessert. Coffee? No soufflés, right? What time would we be home? Sometimes we hadn't even been seated, and he thought we should be on our way home.

"He's just worried," Alicia would reassure me. I knew this, but I still didn't like the double standard. I worried every night about him, too, but I didn't make him feel guilty for coming home late. Maybe I should have suggested he develop a new show called *Double Standard*.

⌘

Aaron loved to tell stories about the real-life characters he'd met. I was more discreet, enjoying watching the show business types in action and "doing their deals." My friend Joyce Kraines suggested I write about "all the amazing people you have had the opportunity to meet." I think I'd need to write a novel if I really wanted to tell the good stories.

⌘

Bill Haber, Aaron's longtime agent, was always teasing us about how hard we both worked and that we never seemed to sleep. When one of us finally fell asleep, the other one would usually find an excuse to wake up our mate.

Bill sent me an e-mail reminding me how Aaron and I would watch CNN and hear stories about people in need, and then spend the rest of the night tracking down information so we could help.

One time, we even paid for a new heart for a teenager. He had played basketball with his friends, and he couldn't do anything because of his bad heart. We had to help. There was so much red tape involved, so we volunteered to be his dieticians, shoppers, and fitness coaches until he could get the new heart. That kind of problem makes sleep seem a lot less important.

※

One of my passions is Mah-Jongg, and my Mah-Jongg buddies are among my closest friends. Many of us have been pals for decades, and the laughter never stops.

Fran Huddleston reminded me of a Mah-Jongg story where my butler, Rodney, went a little overboard. He was, as always, eager to help. During one game, he asked if we needed anything. Fran joked that she needed more jokers. Rodney returned with a bag full of jokers and reported, "Mrs. Spelling keeps these in the bottom drawer."

I realized later that Rodney had gone through all my sets of Mah-Jongg tiles. I told him extra lemonade and cake would have been better.

※

I've written about my holiday party at the end of 2007. Some of my friends wanted to make sure I covered it in my book. I'll sit back and let them take over while I smile proudly.

Paula Kent Meehan, a friend and traveling buddy, wanted to make sure I mentioned the hundreds of toy soldiers on the front steps and the live toy soldiers marching around the fountain.

Linda and Bill Rouse were tickled when they walked in and saw Don Rickles and his wife. They had watched Don's

HBO special the night before. They also liked the bowling and karaoke. "Candy has a beautiful voice and is always humming," Linda told friends. "As we were leaving, I said to Bill, 'I want to show you something.' We went into the doll museum, and sitting on one of the shelves was our original first-grade reading book."

When they left, they told me they wished Aaron had been there to enjoy it. They reminded me that his dream was to see people having that much fun in our home, and Linda said, "I hope he is looking down at us now."

Music was a big part of that night, as it always was in our lives. Sheila Kolker liked the "snow" she could see from the windows, and she reminded me of a fantasy I lived that night:

> The highlight of our night was when all of a sudden the piano player continued to play and Candy stood by his side and proceeded to sing like an angel. Everyone stood around in awe and what was going on in my mind was not only how beautiful she sounded, but how poised and confident she looked. I've known Candy since our boys were little; and as time goes by, we learn more and more about our friend. This was an amazing surprise because I have always admired her grace and elegance, and now I can add to that, a gorgeous voice to match.

Thanks, Sheila, but that was one of the most terrifying things I've ever done. I still can't believe I stood up there and sang. But I wanted to pay tribute to Aaron, so I sang our song, "My Funny Valentine."

�֍

We built The Manor for our family and friends. My friend Darlene Fogel asked that I include in my book one of her "warm fuzzies that I will always remember." We invited her to stay at our home after she had had back surgery. That's what friends do. She later wrote:

> I was sooooooo touched by your warmth and generosity when I shared with you that I was going to have back surgery. Without a thought you said to me, "I want you to stay at my home after the surgery." You and Aaron made me feel so comfortable.

I asked my therapist, Dr. Andrea Brandt, if there was anything she thought I should include or leave out in my book. She offered to explain my humming:

> Her parents taught her manners and threw her lavish birthday parties, but they didn't give her any emotional time. Her response was to hide in her closet and tell herself that her problems were just not important. She felt unloved and unappreciated and not very important to the most important people in her life.
>
> Candy developed a coping mechanism, humming, to serve many purposes: to protect herself, to regulate her feelings,

and it operated as a defense as well as keeping her feelings under wraps. Had her parents been wise enough, they would have realized that the humming was a big clue into how in need she was for their time, attention to her issues.

She still uses humming today, even though she has people who will listen to her. Though she hums less, she uses it now to regulate her stress level.

My closest friends can tell what I'm thinking by what I'm humming and how loudly I hum. That certainly includes Nancy Blumenfeld, my best friend since I was five years old and she was six, and my co-star in *Bop Girl Goes Calypso*, the forgettable 1957 film that cast two giggling, giddy preteens as extras.

Nancy has the most to say about what I should or should not say, not only in the book, but at all times. I guess it's only fair. We've shared some experiences together that make Lucy and Ethel and Laverne and Shirley look like amateur friends.

Nancy reminds me of some of the best times in my life, and things I'd rather forget, like when she and I were put in the 1960s equivalent of "special ed."

Nancy and I were not good readers or particularly good students. Our parents kept us busy with everything "ladylike," such as dancing, etiquette, fashion, cooking, sewing, and charm school. Spelling and math were far down the list. So when we got to high school, our reading, writing, and arithmetic scores were not on par with those of most other students.

Nancy recapped in an e-mail,

We were two bright children with learning disabilities the world knew nothing about. We were labeled "not smart," which was far from the truth and would be proven when we were tested years later. We also found out just recently that Candy had an eye problem, and she saw words in jumbled order.

We would use any excuse we could think of to get out of those classes. It was hard being labeled not smart. In high school they put us in classes with severely disabled students. When it was time for the dismissal bell to ring, we were out the door and across the patio so fast, praying no one would see us coming out of that dreadful classroom.

That heavy weight followed us into adult life. The nice part, if there's anything nice about it, is we shared it together and still do. Candy is one of the brightest people I know. She has always handled all the family business matters very successfully and is a genius at the stock market. In her stock group, everyone listened to her opinions attentively.

I like to think about the good times in high school, such as cooking for my home economics class, but it had its terrible times, too, that destroyed our self-confidence and actually kept us from learning even the most basic subjects.

Candy's mother, Gene, groomed her for a beautiful life. She wanted the best for her daughter, and everyone knew this. She was a beautiful woman with auburn hair and a beautiful model's body and very long manicured nails.

But she slept until three o'clock in the afternoon because she was not well. Everything she did screamed style. Candy was a very obedient, good child. We both demonstrated the best manners when we came in from playing like saying hello as we stood by Gene's bed. She held court there, always dressed in the most beautiful robes. Gene was thoughtful with her brand of the best advice. Everything was manners. Everything. She was very strong on "One never airs dirty laundry in public."

Candy's mother adored her. She was not a demonstrative woman. I never thought that meant she didn't love Candy. She showed her love by trying to do everything possible for Candy, like [buying her] beautiful clothes.

Hey, Nancy? Do you think I can blame my mother for my over-shopping and feeling like I never have enough clothes? Or do all women think they never have anything to wear?

We did have fun in high school. Nancy remembers:

There was always a line of boys waiting to talk to her or take her out.

In our senior year, she was voted best figure and best dressed. I remember sitting in the stands my freshman year in high school, and Candy was on the drill team in a form-fitting outfit and boots. I remember hearing boys asking, who was that new girl.

That was the year of her major transformation, when we started wearing makeup. She had long thick blond hair that she wore in a ponytail halfway down her back, always with rope velvet ribbon to match her outfits. She carried two pictures of herself, "before" and "after," and was proud to show them. She was the star of the home economics department. She could sew and cook. The summer of our freshman year, we took modeling lessons (so we could become more charming!). The school pulled Candy aside because she had the perfect figure and face for modeling. I think her mother nixed it because she was too young.

I don't remember all these compliments, but I hope they're true. Nancy wasn't done. That's understandable, since we have more years together than anyone else:

Tenacity is the word that comes to mind when I think of Candy. She doesn't give up. As a little girl, she lost her skate key in a half acre of thick ivy. Long after I had given up on helping her, she was still outside looking for it until she found it.

I attribute her success in everything she touches to her tenacity. As a child, she was always liked and admired for her beauty and kindness, which she always failed to see. Candy had a magic quality the way she looked at you, with her beautiful riveting pale blue eyes that seemed to be lit [from] within. One was (and still is) drawn in, mesmerized. This is still true today. She was (is) extremely kind and polite, sometimes to the point where one had to say, "Please don't be so polite."

In her home, Candy carries on this tradition. When she entertains, everything is well thought out and everything is focused on the comfort of her guests, like Tori's wedding, where she made each table feel like a small dinner party. The appointments were elegant and tasteful.

Can I add that there has been much said about Candy's gift-wrapping room? Did anyone ever stop to think that the gift-wrap room is part of The Manor because Candy is a giver in life, and nothing pleases her more than giving a gift beautifully wrapped and watching the joy her creativity brings to the face of the recipient?

Thanks, Nancy. We've often said that our friendship has endured so long because of so many shared experiences and because we never felt we had to impress each other or be on our best behavior. We're so fortunate.

Missing from the friends and family who contributed to what they wanted me to say or not say is my daughter, Tori. If Tori would have contributed to my book, my wish would be that she repeat the words of a poem she wrote to me just twelve years ago. It was a beautiful birthday wish, lovingly framed and surrounded by photos of us throughout the years. Her poem, "To My Mother," began:

> *You've been the greatest blessing*
> *In my life, it's clear to see . . .*

She touched my heart when she wrote how she was glad I'm her mother and her friend, how she treasured my faith, love, and hope, and how dear I am to her.

She wrote, "I really appreciate the love / You give without measure."

None of us can measure love, but we can count our blessings. I have many.

Chapter 18

The Pop Culture Trail to Candyland

I think my baby boomer generation grew up during one of the most fascinating, exciting, and confusing times in history, and I wouldn't trade what I've learned and done for anything.

I was born during a time of contradictions. Many celebrated the end of the war that was brought about by the damage and destruction of the atom bomb, while others measured it in terms of human lives and the tragic social and cultural implications. Houses were ninety-nine dollars down and ninety-nine dollars a month, and every child rode his or her bike on the sidewalk in front of houses where bomb shelters were being built in the backyards.

There was a sense of optimism as food rationing and perfume and nylon stocking shortages were coming to an end. (Perhaps this explained my mother's "perfume collection," which rivaled a small store. She always told me, "You don't douse yourself with perfume. Just a little behind your ears and cleavage and nape of your neck. Candy, don't spray it all over.")

And then she would make sure I knew we had to "duck and cover" if and when whoever the bad guys were decided to nuke us back.

We were embarking on times like never before, with innovations in everything from television to underarm deodorant guaranteed not to burn clothes.

Our movie stars were the bravest, our athletes the best, and our dreams the biggest. We were unstoppable.

The messages I received were a bit mixed. I kind of missed the whole hippie thing. I smoked cigarettes, not pot. I sat on love seats, not on the steps of college presidents' offices. I prepared baskets for our troops instead of protesting the draft. It had nothing to do with philosophy or beliefs. When I look at the "red states and blue states" today, I think of the two societies in the 1960s. I was groomed to carry on the traditions of womanhood and motherhood from the 1950s, and the men could take care of "life." While I was going to design college to design how things should look, others were designing how people should *think*. I was brought up to want to join a sorority. Some of my contemporaries worked to make sure such frivolous organizations disappeared. While I worked as a model in fashion layouts for bathing suits and go-go boots, others tried to look like Sonny and Cher before they discovered fashion.

I did make love, not war, but not until I was married, of course, and I got married a month before my eighteenth birthday.

There was no right or wrong path to take. Everyone had his or her own life. I might have liked going to Woodstock to hear the music, but I wouldn't have liked the communal living. In retrospect, I should have cooked for the protesters during their sit-ins.

My growing-up years were a confusing time also in terms of women and working. My fate was clear. I was going to have a womanly career in retail and fashion and then get married. Done. I'd get married. Done. Twice. Then, in between raising children and caring for my husband and home, I could do some charity work. Done. Happily.

If anyone had told me I'd be in charge of insurance and purchasing for one of Hollywood's largest entertainment conglomerates, I would have run the other way. That wasn't in my life plan. Business was all right, as long as it was women's business. Comparing insurance policies and rates? Trying to determine the benefits of health insurance for employees' families? Determining how much our documents were worth in the event of a fire or flood? Purchasing truck-loads of office supplies? Supplies for our wardrobe department? Trucks for our productions? Done it. Take that, June Cleaver and Aunt Bea.

I was also involved in planning and hosting many legendary social and charity events over the years. That was more fun, and closer to my destiny. Just like the Jeffersons, I was moving on up and making sure I was giving back. That's one of the great privileges in life.

And I learned there wasn't anything I couldn't do. Is it any wonder, given that I was brought up with advertising messages that taught me that nothing was out of my reach? Back then we had such information as:

Lysol for feminine hygiene use: I spelled marriage—mirage. A wife's story of marriage happiness rediscovered once her doctor advised her to use Lysol disinfectant for feminine hygiene.

Ouch.

You can give yourself a lovely TONI Home Permanent for your date tonight.

New . . . a cream deodorant which safely helps stop under-arm perspiration. . . . It does not rot dresses and men's shirts.

Does your laxative leave a bad taste in your mouth? Use Ex-Lax, "The Happy Medium Laxative."

Listerine Anti-septic for Infectious Dandruff.

Now that your man is a man of Property and now that you own a house of your very own, use eternally-vigilant Sani-Flush.

I had the added advantage of being named after a movie star, so I had even more information than most about how to act and what I was allowed to do. From one of my mother's magazines came my job description:

> She [Carole Lombard] came down the stairs in a white, satiny robe trimmed with fur like the girls wear in your dreams . . .
>
> She came downstairs in that robe, and if there ever was a million dollars cash she was it.

Television reminded us of all our resources and safety, too. We were in good hands with our insurance company, our imported cars got eighty-four miles per gallon, cheap watches were indestructible, Heinz's slogan told us ketchup was "slow good," we could feel stronger fast with a spoonful of Geritol, lions protected our investments, Ajax cut grease faster and polished with half the effort, even a monkey could operate an early Xerox machine (so women certainly could, I guess), talking tuna and green giants watched over our food, and our FBI agents drove reliable Fords to solve crimes. Slacks and jeans were being allowed for women as "fashion fundamentals to save wear and tear on your best bib and tucker." Vinylite ("new lustrous plastic in a choice of colors never to lose their gleam") handbags had hit the market, as had Sea Nymph bathing suits. We had it all.

We even had hope if we ever messed up. In a 1950 story in *Modern Screen* magazine, Hedda Hopper, the foremost celebrity expert, reported about a new rehabilitation and mental health clinic in Kansas:

> Stars whose emotional mix-ups threaten to wreck their personal lives are facing facts with the aid of science—and finding happiness.

I found happiness, and I know there is so much more to find. What a ride my generation and I have had. And even though we're being called "senior citizens" now (how did that happen?), we've got a lot of teaching, giving, sharing, and experiencing to do.

And I can't wait to create even more stories from Candyland.

Afterword

❧

Writing this book has been one of the most challenging, frightening, and freeing experiences of my life.

My life has always been defined by other people's expectations and dreams, and I was very proud about how much I pleased them. Writing this book flooded me with memories of happy and sad times, but mostly it showed me how far I've come and how far I can still go.

Every day is a new learning experience, with ups and downs, surprises and disappointments, new kinds of fears and new levels of joy.

And now I'm in my sixties and a grandmother. My daughter, Tori, and her husband, Dean, have blessed me with two healthy and beautiful grandchildren, Liam Aaron, born in March 2007, and Stella Doreen, Liam's little sister, born this past June. Randy is great with children and loves being an uncle. He'll be a terrific dad, too.

I can't wait to share my stories and tell my grandchildren of the endless adventures of their wonderful grandfather, make them giggle with stories about their mom growing up, and delight in tales of their Uncle Randy's escapades. In the meantime, though, I'm going to temporarily suspend the baby-talk dialogue we use to communicate and share some thoughts.

Dear Liam and Stella,

I love you, and you have brought so much happiness and meaning to all of us. My only sadness is that you didn't get to meet your grandfather. Oh, would he have loved you! No, make that worship, as he worshipped your mother and uncle.

This is some time to grow up. People have never been exposed to so much, and you will lead relatively sheltered lives, removed from some of the hardships and tragedies of the twenty-first century. I'm relieved we can protect you to some extent, but I don't want you to think you're different or better than anyone else.

I've written about being a celebrity by marriage, and

your mother and uncle were brought up with strangers
smiling at them, sometimes fawning over them, seeking
their approval, giving them whatever they wanted and
asking very little of them. I don't know if that will happen
with you, too, but based on the e-mails and letters I've
received about how beautiful and delightful you both are, I
suspect that you, too, will be the center of attention for much
of your childhood, even before you accomplish anything on
your own.

One of my favorite characters is Auntie Mame (and I
hope you watch that movie when you're older). I'll never
forget her saying, "Live! Life's a banquet and most poor
suckers are starving to death." I always thought it was a
fun way to live, but I realized that Auntie Mame—and my
real-life role models—not only enjoyed the banquet but
helped feed the others and made sure they wouldn't starve.
That's our legacy, that's our privilege, that's what we're
supposed to do. I say to you, "Life's a banquet, and let's
share our blessings with everyone."

I know you'll be Googling and reading all kinds of
stories about our family. Some will make you roll your eyes.
Some will raise questions. Many will be about Charlie's
Angels, Beverly Hills 90210, Dynasty, Fantasy Island, The
Mod Squad, and other titles that won't mean much to you.
I urge you to find the shows, which you'll probably be able to
download into your latest mini-tech-whatever-pod, and see

how your grandfather looked at life, the influences of the generations before you, and what life looked like to your parents and me.

Don't think we were just silly. Things were mostly great and, in relation to today, very simple.

I hope your lives are as happy as ours have been. You are so lucky, have so much potential, and we all love you so much. Please don't grow up too fast. Enjoy your lives and enhance the lives of others, as I do my best to enhance yours.

Love,

Candygram

Candy Spelling's Favorite Recipes

❈

CHICKEN CASSEROLE

• • •

Ingredients

1 cup raw rice

1 fryer, cut up

1 package onion soup, undiluted

1 can beef consommé

1 can cream of mushroom soup, undiluted

1 can water

Preheat oven to 350°F.

Grease a 3-quart casserole dish.

Pour all of the raw rice in the casserole dish, then place the chicken parts on top of the rice. Sprinkle the package of onion soup on top of the chicken, followed by the beef consommé, then the cream of mushroom soup, then 1 can of water.

Do not mix these ingredients.

Place in preheated oven uncovered for 1½ hours. Cover with foil and return to oven for another ½ hour. Remove and serve.

SWISS CHOCOLATE CAKE WITH CHOCOLATE WHIPPED CREAM FROSTING

Ingredients

One 6-ounce package (1 cup) Nestlé chocolate morsels

¼ cup water

2¼ cups flour

1 teaspoon baking soda

¾ teaspoon salt

1¾ cups sugar

¾ cup soft butter

1 teaspoon vanilla

3 eggs

1 cup buttermilk

Preheat oven to 375°F.

Over low heat, melt the chocolate morsels with the water. Set aside.

Sift together the flour, baking soda, and salt. Set aside.

Blend the sugar, butter, and vanilla, then add the eggs one at a time. Stir in the chocolate mixture, and then add the flour mixture, alternating with the buttermilk.

Pour into three greased and floured 8-inch- to 9-inch- layer pans, and bake in preheated oven for 25 to 30 minutes.

CHOCOLATE WHIPPED CREAM FROSTING

Ingredients

- 1 six-ounce package (1 cup) of Nestlé Chocolate Morsels
- 2 tablespoons honey
- 1 teaspoon water
- 3 cups of heavy cream
- ¼ teaspoon instant coffee
- ¼ teaspoon salt

Over low heat, melt chocolate morsels with the honey and water. Mix and cool.

Beat the cream, coffee, and salt until thick.

Fold the cooled chocolate mixture into the whipped cream slowly, and then frost.

MUSHROOM BARLEY SOUP

· · ·

Ingredients

 Turkey carcass

 Celery

 Salt and pepper

 2 cups diced carrots

 2 cups diced celery

 2 packages dried mushrooms, cut up and soaked in water for
   1½ hours

 ¾ cup barley (cooked until done)

 1 can beef consommé (optional)

Cover carcass with water, add celery for flavor, season with salt and pepper, and bring to a boil. Lower heat to simmer. Should produce approximately two quarts (more or less) of broth.

 Strain and add carrots, celery, mushrooms, and barley.

 If darker color is desired, add a can of beef consommé.

· · ·

CANDY SPELLING'S POPOVERS

• • •

Ingredients

  1 cup flour

  ½ teaspoon salt

  1 cup milk

  2 eggs (3 if small)

Preheat oven to 425°F (400°F if using glass).

Sift flour and mix with salt, milk, and eggs. Pour into well-greased deep muffin cups (¾ full) or ramekin (oven-glass cup) (½ full). Bake for 40 to 45 minutes or until golden brown. Serve immediately.

Makes 5 to 9 popovers, depending on size of muffin cups.

Tastes delicious with jam and butter.

• • •

PECAN CRESCENT COOKIES

• • •

Ingredients

- 1 cup pecans (before chopping)
- 1 cup unsifted flour
- 2 tablespoons sugar
- ½ cup butter, softened
- ½ teaspoon vanilla
- Powdered sugar

Preheat oven to 300°F.

Chop pecans finely and set aside. On slow speed, mix in flour, sugar, butter, and vanilla until blended. Add chopped pecans.

Shape into crescents and place on an ungreased cookie sheet. Bake for 40 minutes. Remove from pan to rack placed on paper towels. Sprinkle with powdered sugar when cookies are cool.

• • •

STUFFED ZUCCHINI

Ingredients

3 zucchinis, whole

3 tablespoons butter

1 cup Pepperidge Farm bread stuffing

½ cup cooked tomatoes

salt and pepper

Preheat oven to 350°F.

Boil zucchini whole in salted water for 10 minutes. Cut in halves and scoop out center.

Mix pulp (cut into smaller pieces) with remaining ingredients and fill zucchini shells.

Bake for 15 minutes.

APPLE PIE

• • •

CRUST
Ingredients

  2 cups flour

  ½ to ¾ teaspoon salt

  1 cup Crisco

  ½ teaspoon sugar

  ⅓ cup ice-cold water (as needed)

Mix ingredients together, adding liquid a little at a time as needed, until dough is really mealy, and roll out bottom crust in 9-inch pie pan. Cut crust strips with remaining dough.

FILLING
Ingredients

  ¾ cup sugar

  3 tablespoons Wondra Flour (mix with sugar)

  ½ teaspoon nutmeg

  ½ teaspoon cinnamon

  5 medium Granny Smith apples, sliced

  ¼ cup lemon juice

  ½ cup water

  1 stick butter (¼ for melting)

Combine sugar, flour, nutmeg, and cinnamon. Place 3 table-spoons of these dry ingredients over the bottom crust, then add half the apples. Sprinkle with 2 tablespoons of dry in-gredients, then the remaining apples. Cover with remaining dry ingredients. Pour lemon juice and water. Thin-slice ¾ stick of butter over the top of the pie (reserve ¼).

Place crust strips on top of pie in lattice design and close by pinching ends together.

Cut pieces of foil strips 2 inches wide. Crinkle around edge to prevent burning of pinched ends.

Melt the other ¼ stick of butter and brush top of pie crust. Sprinkle a handful of sugar over whole pie.

Bake at 475°F for about 10 minutes to brown. Reduce heat to 350°F for 45 minutes more, or until apples are soft.

Remove from oven and place on wire rack to cool. Remove crinkle foil from edges.

Serve warm with ice cream or cheddar cheese.

. . .

CORNISH GAME HENS
(MOTHER'S RECIPE)

• • •

Ingredients

6 tablespoons wild rice

5 large mushrooms, separate stems and caps (reserve caps for sauce)

2 stalks celery, diced

1 teaspoon minced onion

2 tablespoons butter

Salt and pepper

4 hens

2 tablespoons soy sauce

Preheat oven to 450°F.

Prepare wild rice. Cut up mushrooms stems. Sauté mushrooms stems, celery, and onion in a little butter. Add salt and pepper. Add to wild rice.

Brush hens all over with butter and the soy sauce and stuff with rice mixture.

Roast for 15 minutes. Reduce heat to 350°F and cook for 30 minutes more.

SAUCE

Ingredients

- 1 small can dark pitted cherries, drained (set aside juice)
- 1 jigger of brandy (optional)
- 5 large mushroom caps (reserved from above)
- 2 teaspoons cornstarch
- ⅔ cup chicken bouillon
- 2 tablespoons red wine
- ¼ teaspoon ginger
- ¼ teaspoon dry mustard
- 3 tablespoons sugar
- 1 tablespoon orange zest

To prepare sauce:

Soak drained cherries in brandy for at least 1 hour. In a small saucepan, mix all the remaining ingredients, and heat slowly until it's the consistency of a glaze. Slice cherries and mushroom caps and sauté in butter, then add to the liquid mixture. Heat and serve over hens.

• • •

SOUR CREAM COFFEE CAKE
WITH PECAN TOPPING

Ingredients

¼ pound butter (1 stick)

1 cup sugar

3 eggs

2 cups sifted flour

1 teaspoon baking powder

1 teaspoon baking soda

½ pint sour cream

½ cup white raisins

Preheat oven to 350°F.

Cream butter and sugar thoroughly. Add eggs one at a time, beating well after each addition. Sift together flour, baking powder, and baking soda. Add to creamed mixture, alternating with sour cream and blending after each addition. Mix in raisins.

Spread the mixture in a greased and floured 13-by-9-by-2-inch baking pan. Sprinkle with pecan topping. Bake for 35 to 40 minutes.

PECAN TOPPING

Ingredients

¾ cup brown sugar

1 tablespoon flour

1 teaspoon cinnamon

2 tablespoons butter

1 cup chopped pecans

Combine sugar, flour, and cinnamon. Cut in butter, then add nuts and mix.

CHOCOLATE CUPCAKES

Ingredients

4 squares semisweet chocolate

2 sticks sweet butter

1½ cups chopped pecans

1 cup flour

1¾ cups sugar

4 eggs

1 teaspoon vanilla

Powdered sugar

Preheat oven to 325°F.

Melt chocolate and butter. Add nuts and stir. Set aside. Combine by hand the flour, sugar, eggs, and vanilla, and blend. Stir in chocolate. Do not beat.

Pour into muffin tins lined with paper cups. Bake for 35 minutes. Cool and sprinkle with powdered sugar.

NOTE: Fill muffin papers ¾ full and at 30 minutes test with a toothpick. When baked, put entire muffin tin on wire rack, not on the counter. Do not sprinkle with powdered sugar until completely cool.

COLD LEMON SOUFFLÉ
(LOW CALORIE)

• • •

Ingredients

>   4 egg whites
>
>   ½ cup water
>
>   1 cup nonfat milk powder
>
>   ½ cup fructose
>
>   1½ tablespoons unflavored Knox gelatin
>
>   ½ cup lemon juice
>
>   2 drops yellow food coloring
>
>   1 lemon peel, grated

Beat egg whites, water, powdered milk, and fructose until stiff. In a saucepan, heat Knox gelatin and lemon juice over low heat. Do not boil. Add 2 drops food coloring. When gelatin is completely dissolved, remove from heat and fold in egg-white mixture. Once mixed, add lemon peel. Pour into individual pot-au-crème or custard cups. Refrigerate until chilled and set. Should have the consistency of cold soufflé.

PEANUT BUTTER PILLOWS

In this recipe, peanut butter is sandwiched between two peanut butter icebox cookies and then the cookies are baked. The cookies are crisp; the filling is soft.

Ingredients

1½ cups sifted all-purpose flour

½ teaspoon baking soda

¼ teaspoon salt

¼ pound (1 stick) butter

½ cup smooth (not chunky) peanut butter

½ cup sugar

¼ cup light corn syrup

1 tablespoon milk

Additional peanut butter for filling (scant ½ cup)

Sift together the flour, baking soda, and salt and set aside. In the small bowl of an electric mixer, cream the butter. Add the peanut butter and sugar and beat until thoroughly mixed. Beat in the corn syrup and milk. On low speed, add the sifted dry ingredients, scraping the bowl as necessary with a rubber spatula and beating only until smooth.

Turn the dough out onto a lightly floured large board or a smooth work surface. Knead it briefly and then, with your hands, form it into an even roll or oblong, about 7 inches long and 2¼ to 2½ inches in diameter. Wrap the dough in wax paper, slide a cookie sheet underneath, and transfer the dough to the refrigerator for several hours, or longer if you wish.

Adjust the oven racks to divide the oven into thirds and preheat oven to 350°F.

With a sharp knife, cut half of the roll of dough into slices ⅛- to ¼-inch thick. Place the slices 2 inches apart on ungreased cookie sheets.

Place 1 level measuring teaspoonful of the additional peanut butter in the center of each cookie. Then spread the peanut butter only slightly to flatten it, leaving a ½- to ¾-inch border.

Slice the remaining half of the roll of dough (same thickness), and as you cut each slice, place it over one of the peanut-butter-topped cookies. Let the cookies stand for 2 or 3 minutes, allowing the dough to soften slightly. Then seal the edges by pressing them lightly with the back of the tines of the fork, dipping the fork in flour as necessary to keep it from sticking. (Don't worry about slight cracks in the tops.)

Bake for 12 to 15 minutes, reversing the position of the cookie sheets top to bottom and front to back to ensure even browning.

RED VELVET CAKE

Ingredients

½ cup shortening (Crisco)

1½ cups sugar

2 eggs

½ ounce red food dye (fill glass measuring cup with 2½ ounces of water, to make 3 ounces)

2 tablespoons unsweetened cocoa

1 teaspoon salt

2¾ cups flour, unsifted

1 cup buttermilk

1 teaspoon vanilla

1 tablespoon white vinegar

1 teaspoon baking soda

Preheat oven to 350°F.

Cream shortening and sugar, and add eggs. In a separate

bowl make a paste of the food coloring, water, and cocoa. Add this to the creamed mixture. Add salt to the flour and stir into the creamed mixture, alternating with the buttermilk. Add the vanilla. Mix the vinegar and baking soda together in a separate container and let fizz, then blend into the other ingredients.

Pour into two 8-inch-layer pans that have been greased and floured and bake for 30 minutes.

ICING

Ingredients

> 5 tablespoons flour
>
> 1 cup whole milk
>
> 1 cup butter (do not use margarine)
>
> 1 cup sugar
>
> 1 teaspoon vanilla

Over a low flame, cook the flour and milk (stir while cold, so it won't form lumps) until thickened. Watch carefully; this is fast. When pasty, remove from heat and place pan in a sink of cold water to cool. While cooling, cream the butter and sugar, adding the vanilla last. Add flour mixture and beat about 15 minutes, or until creamy.

• • •

CHEESE PIE

. . .

CRUST

Ingredients

> 16 graham crackers, rolled fine
>
> ½ stick melted butter
>
> 2 tablespoons sugar
>
> Dash of cinnamon

In a large bowl, mix all the ingredients and press into pie pan. Bake for 8 minutes.

FILLING

Ingredients

> 3 small packages (or 1 large +1 small) cream cheese, softened
>
> 2 eggs
>
> ½ cup sugar
>
> 1 teaspoon vanilla

Preheat oven to 350°F.

Beat ingredients together and pour into pie crust. Bake for 20 minutes.

TOPPING
Ingredients

   1 pint sour cream

   8 teaspoons sugar

   2 teaspoons vanilla

Whip together sour cream, sugar, and vanilla. Spread on pie, which has been removed from oven. Return to oven for 5 minutes more. Cool, then refrigerate.

THUMBPRINT COOKIES

Ingredients

   ½ pound butter

   ½ cup sugar

   3 egg yolks

   3 cups flour

   Jam of choice

Preheat oven to 350°F.

   Cream butter and sugar well. Add 1 egg yolk at a time and mix well. Then add flour.

   Roll in balls and press well on a cookie sheet, leaving a well in the middle with your thumb. Bake for 20 minutes. Fill center well with jam while still warm.

CARROT CAKE
WITH CREAM CHEESE FROSTING

Ingredients

2½ cups flour

2 cups sugar

1 teaspoon baking soda

½ teaspoon salt

1⅓ cups vegetable oil (not butter or margarine)

3 eggs

1 teaspoon vanilla

Approximately 2 cups grated carrots

1 cup chopped walnuts

Preheat oven to 350°F.

Sift together flour, sugar, baking soda, and salt. In a separate bowl, cream together oil and eggs. Add dry ingredients to wet ingredients. Mix well. Add vanilla, carrots, and nuts, mixing in well.

Pour cake batter into Bundt pan or ungreased angel food cake pan and bake for 1 hour, or until top is crusty and toothpick inserted in center comes out clean.

CREAM CHEESE FROSTING

Ingredients

> One 8-ounce package cream cheese, softened
>
> 1 box powdered sugar

Combine cream cheese and sugar until smooth. Spread on cake once it is cooled.

CIOPPINO

Ingredients

> 1 large sea bass
>
> 1 large raw lobster
>
> 1 large raw Dungeness crab
>
> 1 pint mussels
>
> 1 pint Little Neck clams (reserve strained liquid)
>
> ½ cup dried mushrooms
>
> ½ cup olive oil
>
> 1 large chopped onion
>
> 2 cloves garlic, minced
>
> 3 tablespoons chopped parsley
>
> 1 large green pepper, chopped
>
> 1 generous cup cooked tomatoes

1 bay leaf

Salt to taste

Cayenne, to taste

1 cup shelled uncooked shrimp

Slice sea bass, cut lobster into pieces, and break raw Dungeness crab into pieces. Wash thoroughly 1 pint *each* of the mussels and Little Neck clams and steam them open. Reserve the strained liquid.

Soak the mushrooms in water until their original size and chop into small pieces.

Heat olive oil in a large iron pan. Add onion, garlic, parsley, green pepper, and the chopped mushrooms. Cook mixture over low flame for about 5 minutes, stirring frequently. Add cooked tomatoes, bay leaf, and the reserved liquid from clams and mussels. Cover pan and simmer for 1 hour.

Season with salt and cayenne pepper.

Add sea bass, lobster, crab, and the shrimp and cook for 15 or 20 minutes without stirring. Finally, add mussels and clams and heat them through. Serve in heated soup plates or bowls.

AARON'S FAVORITE FRIED CHICKEN

• • •

Ingredients

> 3-pound chicken, cut into 8 pieces
>
> ¼ cup salt
>
> Salt and pepper to taste
>
> 1 cup flour
>
> Enough neutral-flavored vegetable oil to come up to ½ inch in
>> your frying pan

Soak chicken overnight in salt water. Rinse in fresh water and pat each piece very dry. Lightly salt and pepper each piece. Drop in a bag of flour to coat. Remove as much of the flour as possible. Heat vegetable oil in skillet till bubbling, add chicken carefully to avoid splashes, cover and cook for 20 to 25 minutes (about 10 minutes on each side), or until crispy and golden.

• • •